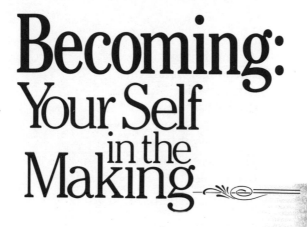

Becoming:
Your Self
in the
Making

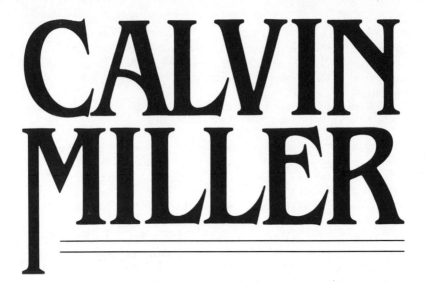

Becoming:
Your Self
in the
Making

Fleming H. Revell Company
Old Tappan, New Jersey

Scripture quotations identified NIV are from the HOLY BIBLE: NEW INTERNATIONAL VERSION. Copyright © 1978 by the International Bible Society. Used by permission of Zondervan Bible Publishers.
Scripture quotations identified NAS are from the New American Standard Bible, © The Lockman Foundation 1960, 1962, 1963, 1968, 1971, 1972, 1973, 1975, 1977.
Scripture quotations identified KJV are from the King James Version of the Bible.

Lines from "Wisdom" reprinted with permission of Macmillan Publishing Company from COLLECTED POEMS by Sara Teasdale. Copyright © 1917 by Macmillan Publishing Company, renewed 1945 by Mamie T. Wheless.
Lines from MIND SONG reprinted by permission of the author, Donna Swanson, R.1, Williamsport, Indiana.
Lines from "The Farmer and the Cowman Should be Friends" by Richard Rodgers and Oscar Hammerstein II copyright © 1943 by Richard Rodgers and Oscar Hammerstein II. Copyright renewed, Williamson Music Co., owner of publication and allied rights. International copyright secured. ALL RIGHTS RESERVED. Used by permission.
Verses from *Going Home* by Judith Deem Dupree are used by permission. *Going Home* is distributed by Baker Book House.
Verses from "I'm Gonna Sit Here," by James Kavanaugh are from *Laughing Down Lonely Canyons*, copyright © 1984. Published by Harper & Row, Publishers, Inc.
"I-ness" by Calvin Miller is from *When the Aardvark Parked on the Ark*, copyright © 1984. Published by Harper & Row, Publishers, Inc.

Library of Congress Cataloging in Publication Data

Miller, Calvin.
    Becoming : your self in the making.

    Bibliography: p.
    1. Self. 2. Christian life—1960–
I. Title.
BF697.M515   1987   158'.1   86-31323
ISBN 0-8007-1522-5

Copyright © 1987 by Calvin Miller
Published by the Fleming H. Revell Company
Old Tappan, New Jersey 07675
Printed in the United States of America

Contents

Introduction

The search for ourselves is lifelong. My hope is that this book will become the companion of your own personal quest for self-understanding.

This book will not attempt to tell you how to succeed or how to deal with inferiority. It will not tell you "how to do" anything. It is not a book about doing, but about becoming. The probability is that when you know who you are, you will know what to do.

The assertion of this book is that your view of yourself issues from all you produce. But it is equally true that all that comes from your life becomes the definition of who you are. What you are is always more than what you produce. Yet all things, material or physical, emotional or psychological, relational or poetic, artistic or practical, that issue from your being become the way you know yourself and the visible part of the self you show to others.

If what comes from your life is etched by the definition of who you are, to see it and understand is to affirm not just your reality, but your worth to God, your world, and yourself. Read and discover and celebrate the making of yourself.

CALVIN MILLER
Omaha, Nebraska

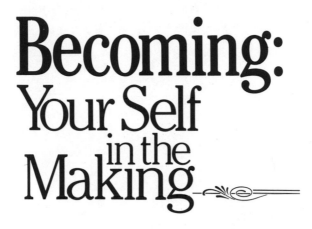
Becoming:
Your Self
in the
Making

1

What You Make Is Who You Are

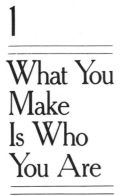

 Experience is not transmissible.

Samuel Taylor Coleridge

This is the true joy in life, the being used for a purpose recognized by yourself as a mighty one; the being a force of nature instead of a feverish selfish little clod of ailments and grievances complaining that the world will not devote itself to making you happy.

George Bernard Shaw, *Man and Superman*

There are vast tracts of undeveloped life in most of us. We have capacities for creativity, for love and for accomplishment that lie fallow. We are dormant in our personal relationships and get pushed around unconscionably. We are timid in our work and get passed over for promotions. We are intimidated in our marriages and get used. We feel futile in our communities, fated to shabby and shoddy service from government and business.

Then, from time to time, a person stands up among us and announces how marvelous it is to simply be human.

Eugene H. Peterson, *Earth and Altar*

Several years before Gutzon Borglum sculpted Mount Rushmore, he was challenged to carve the American presidents on ivory toothpicks. He declined, saying that no matter how exquisite or intricate, "toothpick presidents" do not intrigue. Littleness may pique our interest, but only greatness enthralls.

Borglum, dreaming greatness, picked up his tools. As he approached the mountain for the first time, did he have second thoughts? Hanging like a spider on Mount Rushmore, did he sometimes question that his dream of greatness might be fraught with pain and disappointment? Mountains yield slowly, even to mighty imaginations. The granite mountain, at times, seemed manganese, destroying his drill points by the thousands. In the early days of his work, money was scarce and no federal funds were available. The Jefferson face, begun to the left of the gigantic Washington head, was streaked with unstable granite and had to be destroyed and begun again to the right.

Borglum himself was aging as he began the work in 1927 and must have suspected he would never live to see it completed. He would never live to behold the final polishing of his monument. His years always protested his dream. His back, bent over heavy air hammers and steel drills, challenged his stamina. He must have resented the towering ice facade of Mount Rushmore when frost glazed the stone. Now he is gone, but not his mountain. Who is not overwhelmed by his vision? Who is not inspired by the finished dreams of great dreamers?

Borglum was an artist: a maker. But in those lonely moments—scaffolded to the sky—what was he really making? Presidents? I suppose so. But in a very real sense he was making Borglum!

Whatever we seek to fashion in life becomes the definition of ourselves. And the size of our creative dreams measures also the greatness of our own souls.

Dreams always precede reality. Dreams undergird our vision and become "the target that beckons."[1] How true is that easily read epigram towering over Disney's Epcot: "If you can dream it, you can do it."[2]

In what way are you like the mountain sculptor? You are both the size and quality of those dreams that drive you.

The Driving Dream

It is probably true that most of the men and women you admire do not create anything on the same gargantuan scale that Borglum did. Still, you are a human being and all humankind is dream driven. Consider the various kinds of creative genius that mark our world. Mary Cassatt's marvelous use of color and light seemed to illuminate her canvases from behind. Tolstoi struggled through at least nine Russian longhand drafts of *War and Peace*. Jonas Salk gave us freedom from the fear of polio. Einstein wrapped matter and energy together in a short, three-letter formula. Emily Dickinson sang in solitude and her impeccable literature gave to her the title, the Belle of Amherst.

But does what you create in life have to be as artistic as mountain sculptures or novels? Certainly not! There are many kinds of product. Product can be spiritual. Was not Hudson Taylor, the missionary, also a great creator and a great soul? He fashioned of China a continent of God-lovers. Francis of Assisi reshaped the mountain of class religion by challenging the unfeeling politics of self-serving priests.

There are many kinds of simple, domestic product. You may hold the important career of motherhood, for instance. You may see your children as the unshaped gift of God, the most significant kind of product that can issue from any life.

Product

In writing this book, I longed for a synonym for *product* with a less tangible ring to it. I wanted a word that was not so harsh and one-dimensional. I wanted a word that was not so material. I have not found any better word to stand for that which issues from our being and becomes the outer definition of our inner being and purpose. So let's take a minute and widen this word to the place it may apply to all. Product: the counselor's art. Product: a thousand acres of chocolate furrows cut by the farmers' plows. Product: a well-delivered sermon working inside an unknowable life. Product: the character of a parent whose very mental image shares a child's life. Product: not money, sometimes not material enough to be subject to any of our fine scales, but *real value emanating from our lives and defining who we are.*

Let us build this book on your sense of responsibility. You are a steward of whatever vision orders your life. Making your dreams come true arouses your discipline and orders you out of bed on tired mornings. Why do you get up at the sound of the sassy alarm? You are off to the making of something. There is no doubt about it! You are a maker! In the arts, inward life, in faith, in politics, in sociology, science, industry, agriculture, education, business, or homemaking, you create and thus become!

To make is a primal drive. Lao-tzu reminded us that the greatest of leaders not only found pride in what they created but also inspired those around them to be creators as well.

> *But of a good leader, who talks little,*
> *When his work is done, his aim fulfilled,*
> *They will all say, "We did this ourselves."*[3]

How important—how altogether essential—it is for you to be able to say, "See, this is 'of me' or 'from me'—I did it! Me!" The treasure of your accomplishment is the foundation of your self-esteem.

Maurice Wagner, in *The Sensation of Being Somebody* (Zondervan, 1975), sees "three legs" to the stool of self-esteem. First, says Wagner, you must be loved or self-esteem is impossible. Next, you must feel worthy: Worthiness comes because you believe that who you are and what you do is right. Finally, you must feel capable: You must believe within yourself that you can accomplish your dreams and goals. While there is much to be said for Wagner's view, I believe it is the sense of product that creates in us a sense of both love and worthiness.

I will deal later with the love that grows from the esteem of others. At this point I need to say that our earliest self-esteem is rooted in the esteem of our parents. This esteem becomes the prime motivator for loving ourselves. When we are small children, our product appears good only because we have not developed our sense of mature judgment. Still, our parents' celebration of what we produce furnishes us a feeling of being loved and therefore gives rise to our own self-love. It also makes us feel we are capable of producing something else that earns us more approval and, therefore, more self-love, and so on.

Hence, again and again, the whole issue of your own self-esteem attaches itself to what you produce. Make no mistake about it. What you produce—both in quality and amount—will sooner or later foster self-esteem. Therefore, you must produce something or you will never be able to sustain a quality view of all you are. This is true of individuals and whole societies.

In *The Ascent of Man,* Jacob Bronowski wrote: ". . . every man, every civilization, has gone forward because of its engagement with what it has set itself to do."[4] Our doing is us!

Romance With a Big Chief Tablet

It was probably back in the first grade that I discovered the premise of this book. My mother gave me two objects with which I shared a glorious communion: a simple penny pencil and a Big Chief tablet. It was her intention that I use the tablet to write my ABCs, and so I did. But there were, after all, only twenty-six letters, fifty-two if you counted lowercase; seventy-eight once you learned cursive. What intrigued me was not letters, which fit very neatly between the sea-blue lines, but the easy way graphite rubbed off the pencil point and onto the paper.

Soon my pencil flew in contempt of those twenty-six lines. A tree spilled off my pencil point, intersecting the defiant blue parallel lines with glory. Down, down, down the page ran the lead-line trunk while graphite branches lifted up, up, up. I had never felt such joy! It was a Big Chief landscape—written where an alphabet was meant to go. And there was so much lead in a pencil! So much paper in a tablet! So much space on a page! And there was time—after all, it takes almost no time to write an *A* or a *B* or a *C*. And if I hurried, I could draw a meadowlark or Miss Durksen's desk or Chapman's Grocery across the street from my first-grade classroom, or the steam locomotive whose whistle was a constant, shrill serenade on our end of town.

It was all so wonderful!

Except for the lines—the obscenity of Big Chief tablets! Rigid! Determined! Blue! Mindlessly parallel! Splitting every beautiful picture into twenty-six stiff segments. There was no way to get the lines off the page, so my eye must erase. My mind must "ungeometry" the page. Then I could run in breathlessly and say, "Look, Mommy—look what I made!"

"Look to your ABCs, son! Tablets are expensive!"

"Here they are, Mom!"

And sure enough, they were there: my ABCs scattered around the branches of my landscape or filling the sky above Chapman's Grocery or twined into the smoke of the locomotive that had shrilled the air around Miss Durksen's insistence that *A*'s should not be drawn with long pretty tails, even if there was plenty of time to do so. The tails on my *A*'s were not necessarily pretty and didn't fit in the Big Chief lines, she said.

I scarcely learned my ABCs that year, but it was a year of great discovery! I made things—beautiful things—as I reckoned beauty! My *A*'s still had tails on them, but so did kites and tails seemed appropriate to both!

It was Miss Hill in the fourth-grade art class who introduced me to plain white paper. She gave me such a big sheet! And tempera! I exploded with joy when she handed me a brush. The Big Chief tablet joy had come again—without any lines! My fingers dipped the brush. Paint as blue as the robin's egg in my pocket-knife box flowed from the brush and onto the pure white. I had never been fishing but I had always wanted to go. I did! I painted myself in blue pants and a straw hat. It was a glorious day! My brush flew at Miss Hill's begging paper! My tongue twisted in my cheek and made a perceptible point of pink at the corner of my mouth (a habit I have never shaken each time I yet pick up a brush).

I painted a pond and hung a fishing line down into it.

I pulled fish from the hook and put them in the creek and redipped my brush and painted more. It was my first time ever to fish and I caught many. I dipped my brush into the yellow and my straw hat turned gold in the Oklahoma sun. A little bird flew onto the page and perched in sparrow brown on a green-tempera weed to watch.

"That's very good!"

It was Miss Hill.

She was right! It was very good.

"Class, look what Calvin has done!"

She hung the picture in front of the class. I was ecstatic! She put a little card frame around it and sent it to the county fair. It won a ribbon! It went from there to a national contest. She said I might win there, too. I never did! But I envisioned the picture in a great gallery with chubby men in tuxedos squinting at it through monocles and remarking how very fine it was!

How glorious was this early view of what I had made!

If I should come across that early art, there is little doubt in my mind I would now think it poor. Doesn't maturity always deliver us to better judgment? It also delivers us to finer art and more exquisite taste. But it does not deliver us from the yearning to make something.

The Innate Self and the Quantum Self

The innate self is so inward it remains undefined. This DNA, image-of-God self is our unknowable, untestable self. It is our real but completely undisclosed self. No one can cross the threshold to our real but hidden selves.

The quantum self, on the other hand, is more outward and therefore more measurable. "See," it cries, "here I am. The visible me is the evidence of my reality. I am physical enough to take up space in my world. My quantum self emanates from my innate self—it is my seeable self with all that it produces. In my quantum self are a thousand more objective evidences of my being."

The word *quantum* implies measurement—something to be weighed, observed, recorded: the outer and measurable things that proceed from our lives. The quantum self is the definition that can be written down—the list of all we have done, been, photographed, and collected. All that issues from ourselves in visible ways is added together and tabulated by those who can claim to know who we are. The final sum of such outward assessment adds up to our quantum self.

It would be years between that first eager day of the Big Chief tablet and my discovery of Ayn Rand's truism: Art is man defining himself. We are all artists in our right. Butchers, bakers, candlestick makers: All are makers. Each needlepoint, skyscraper, or toothpick cottage originates from inside ourselves. They not only come from inside us, but they tell us who we are. The pinewood-derby entry and the Eiffel Tower both define something fundamental about their maker. Like God, we are makers.

This book presupposes that the self exists in two modes. The earliest and most primal self is what I shall refer to in the rest of this book as the innate self.

As what you make tells us about your quantum self, creation tells you of God. You are His workmanship (Ephesians 2:10). I marvel that after each of the days of creation, God says in King James glory—"It is good!" And deserving artist that He is, God wrote His name in every part of His paradise. He signed "God" on every leaf mixed into every forest. Every feather of a hummingbird bears His single celebration and signature, "This I made and it is good, God."

Theologians talk about God in these same two modes. God exists in His mysterious hiddenness. In His hiddenness, He is unknowable. But God, as He reveals Himself, in nature can be seen and known in His "quantum self." Saint Paul says that this quantum God causes us to know there is a hidden God from which the revealed one emanates (Romans 1:20).

According to the Bible, the last creative act of God, the great Maker, was to make Adam, a lesser maker. And are you not his grandchild? About to be caught naked, Adam made fig-leaf garments. His grandchildren made deerskin loincloths; later on, his great-great-grandchildren made carded-wool togas and, finally his ever so great-grandchildren made Orlon jumpsuits.

Adam sired a race of makers. Great pharaohs dreamed morbid dreams of big tombstones and watched with pride as they moved the last heavy capstones to the top of pyramids. Of course, they smiled and said, "That's good." The ancient cave painters in Altamira, Spain, labored in the dark cavern's heart under flickering orange flames with gray smoke distorting all but their determination. The swarthy, grunting artist smiled and, tearing a chunk of dog meat from the spit, said in Neanderthal grunts, "Pretty good!" Was it not his moment with a pencil and Big Chief tablet? Whatever we make that is good we survey with the blessing of our own self-esteem. "It's good!" becomes a declaration.

When you were a child, you may have rushed in with a picture of a stick cowboy on a fat Crayola pony. What really occurred as your mother put it under a magnetized ladybug on the icebox door? Was there a celebration in the kitchen? Did the celebration affirm you? But didn't the celebration really create you as it affirmed you? Remember, God celebrated what He had made in Genesis. This same blessing was common to Pharaoh Khufu or the Spanish aborigines. You were wholesome and right in your childhood when you showed your mother the picture and said, "It's good, isn't it, Mommy!"

Most of your childhood self-esteem rose from the making of things—the arts and crafts kind of self-definition. Later psychology and philosophy pried open the narrowness of your world. The word *make* grew wider than mere artifacts. Then you could see there were not only picture makers or statue makers or house makers, but there were idea makers, psychotherapy makers, social-harmony makers, political-change makers. These kinds of nonmaterial creations also deserved the same modifier, spoken with the same ego gratification, "That's good!" Producing intangible or material realities, you defined your quantum self, and spoke of the innate being out of which your own self was becoming defined.

The Cinderella Saturation

Self-esteem is now a trendy term! Yet, no one can doubt its importance! Television lecturers tell you to think well of yourself. Narcissus counsels you to put on a new view of yourself and out-glitter, out-proud, out-intimidate, out-positive-think the dullard world around you. The problem is that everyone in the dullard world around you reads the same books and tries to create himself or herself into a Cinderella.

The Cinderella syndrome is an example of what happens when the quantum self is allowed to exist with little reference to the innate self. Narcissus cares little about what he really is, only how he appears and how he gets on in the world.

When the whole society is narcissistic, it must of necessity be plastic, where automatons, with no real disclosure of themselves, live with their quantum Cinderella side to the camera. They are, in short, only camera people, knowable only as they can be seen. Their innate selves are not treasured and in most cases never acknowledged.

How much room is there in the world for such Cinderellas? The human census is exploding. The race will double in twenty-five years. Demographers forecast that our world will have to make space for 7.2 billion by the end of this present century.[5] The very size of your world may make it hard for you to find a pumpkin to furnish your coach. You may wish to join the ranks of the Cinderellas. You may challenge them, confront them, compete against them, adore them, abhor them, denigrate, or celebrate them. You may even envy them. But the actual number of rags-to-riches beauty queens that any culture can absorb is limited. We may at present be very close to the "Cinderella saturation" point. You may have to face the facts; only a few "Ellas" are called from the "cinders" to marry princes. Most marry chimney sweeps or die spinsters in old fireplaces.

But what can you do if you are a contemporary "Ella" determined to leave the "cinders"? It's all a matter of self-discipline, say the promoters. You can do it if . . . if you learn the public relationalism of Dale Carnegie . . . if you enroll in Toastmasters . . . if you can become a real "live Ringer," you can win through intimidation; you can then bully your fairy godmother into glass Guccis and a spare pumpkin. You must believe in the one great truth at the heart of the self-help revolution: Everyone can be a Cinderella.

The theme of every self-esteem best-seller declares you can do it! But is this an honest assumption?

I remember as a pastor preaching on the commandment, "Sell all you have and give it to the poor."

"Is this commandment for everyone?" grumbled a wealthy but stingy member after services.

"Yes, of course," I said.

"Impossible," he objected.

"Why so?" I asked.

"If *everyone* in all the world sold all they had, who would buy it?"

I have wondered about the challenge of motivators. If everyone were a Cinderella, who would make the glass slippers? No, whatever the motivator's promise, there is a Cinderella saturation point.

Further, the insinuation also slurs over individual competency. Is everyone capable of being a Cinderella? Is there, inside every assembly-line dropout, a Lee Iacocca? Do the bristling sideburns of every Dagwood Bumstead house a Mr. Dithers? Can every soul starved for self-esteem find deliverance in the pages of a self-help book? I think not! You cannot merely read and think well of yourself. Self-esteem is never self-made! It grows from the esteem of others, given in response to all our lives produce.

To Produce Is the Road and the Goal

One contemporary positivist has called self-esteem a *new* reformation, but I wonder. The search for self-esteem is really an old pursuit and as such is not a "reformation" at all. It has been a compelling issue in every age. Popular self-help schemes may promise shortcuts to success. But thinking well of yourself is not a push-pull, click-click issue. You cannot gird up your sagging esteem and smile a new self-evaluation into being. You cannot, in all likelihood, glitter on command. You must produce something that wins you outer esteem so you can arrive at inner esteem.

"To produce" is both the road and the goal to self-esteem. The old adage "Build a better mousetrap and the world will beat a path to your door" is true. They will not come to your door to tell you how much they esteem you. They will come to your door to buy a mousetrap.

The whole issue of how a great mousetrap builder perceives himself has to do totally with his traps. Does he build a good trap? Does it lure the most wary of mice to its waiting jaws? Does it load lightly, require only a little cheese, demand no upkeep, and generally convince a mousy householder that it is necessary? If all of these things are true then, of course, the builder of such a trap becomes the *Fortune* magazine honoree, the man of the year!

The important thing to remember is that he did not set out to become the man of the year. He set out to build a good trap. From him came a touchable, observable product that made the world think well of him and, consequently, he thought better of himself.

Struggle is a marvelous harmonizer. It causes the quantum self to ask the question "Why will the world not see the beautiful and valuable product that is from myself?" In this unsatisfied desire to be appreciated, the innate self grows in wisdom and understanding. Lack of esteem given by the outer world matures and makes wise the innate self.

It should be noted that the quantum self and the innate self rarely grow at the same time. As the quantum self is celebrated, it often grows arrogant and ever ruthless in the world it feels it has a right to control. In such cases, the inner self atrophies from neglect. On the other hand where the quantum self is ignored or despised, we feel hurt and retreat inward thus beginning to esteem our innate self which is being fashioned by pain into wisdom. In this constant tension between the quantum self and the innate self, our humanity is born.

But sometimes our struggle to produce ends up teaching us only humility. Some artists, poets, and writers, for instance, may never have the world beat a path to their door. The same is sometimes true of the "butcher, the baker, and candlestick maker." These small businessmen may find their dreams fading and they may at last board up their shops in insolvency. To these, esteem comes slowly. They sometimes die in the confusion between the confidence that what they have produced really was good and the unsatisfied hunger that few ever said so. So it is not just affirmation that produces self-esteem, but strong faith in the quality of our yet-to-be-affirmed product. In such lives the dream in self is all-important and affirms our uncelebrated worth. We must never, therefore, surrender our dream or allow it to be bought or crushed.

Buying, Selling, Enduring

But you must beware! Great dreams can be sold cheaply. A friend of mine says that Satan buys despairing futures. He is a black-market merchant, eagerly bartering with the discouraged. He buys low and sells high each despairing dream. He will not buy any soul, for he knows that the purchase of a soul destroys only one person. The purchase of a dream, however, may destroy a world.[6]

Even if you have determined not to sell out, you must yet beware! If Satan cannot buy your dreams, his ploy is to crush them: What he cannot buy he will seek to destroy by making the way to your dreams difficult or impossible. They are often abandoned because the road to their fulfillment is a *Via Do-*

lorosa of crushed hopes and despair. Dreams are hard to keep alive, and the rocky road to their fulfillment may bring pain!

Still, pain is the very stuff of sensitivity in life. Further, it is a built-in factor of quality control in what you make. As you swelter in suffocating criticism, you reexamine life and product; then you find a better way to do it and your product improves. To have no problems en route to achievement can allow you to be entangled in cheap success. Cheap success makes too much of the fast prize. Cheap success struts, brags, and becomes a god to itself. It could end in the smallest of all events: the tiny celebration of yourself. The old cliché "God be with you, but not too soon" was born in the interest of saving you from yourself.

The meaning you find in life will be rooted in your own self-esteem, just as who you are is related to the issue of what you produce. Descartes is famous for saying, *Cogito ergo sum*, "I think, therefore I am." What he meant is this: Your ability to reflect tells you that you exist. It is sometimes easier "to be," however, than to like what you are.

Self-reflection alone cannot bring quality to being. Self-reflection can be critical or morose. It is even suicidal at times. Is it not equally true to say, *Facio ergo sum*, "I make therefore I am"? If this statement seems audacious, remind yourself of the mood so common among the disconsolate and the depressed: "What have I really ever done, what have I made, what have I ever produced? Nothing! Nothing! Nothing! There is a huge zero in the center of my existence!"

But even zeros are a kind of product. A suicide note is produced and often is a masterpiece of creativity. Such plaintive memos are etchings of the tension between our quantum and innate selves. Hamlet, for instance, contemplating suicide, waxes eloquent: "To be or not to be." Of course, Shakespeare's Hamlet is fictional, but there have been many real persons who have left behind eloquent notes. The artist Barton laments that he had run from wife to wife all in a desperate attempt to escape from himself. James Forrestal's suicide note was taken from these words of Sophocles:

> *When reason's day*
> *Sets rayless, joyless, quenched in cold decay,*
> *Tis better to die than linger on*
> *And dare to live when the soul's life is gone.*

Did not Forrestal meticulously select just the right words to mark his dying? Did he not weigh the impact they would bear upon the unsuspecting nation? Did he not even envision the four-inch headlines? Even as he wore the final heaviness of his search, did he not reach out with power and significant product—his majestic farewell?

Where did Forrestal really err?

To feel as though your dreams are nothing is a denial of all God made you to be—a producer. You must not allow yourself to deny your origin in the creativity of God. You must cling in faith to the very existence of your innate self. From your innate self derives the traceable, quantum self. You exist as a maker. In both of these selves is the treasure of self-esteem that forbids you to grovel in despair.

When you find yourself despairing, how do you rise from these depths to a reborn faith?

How to Measure the Validity of Your Dreams

To this point, we have fixed this truth: Product (what you make) roots itself in your dreams. How can you determine if your dreams are valid? Here are four principles for determining the validity of your dreams.

First, your dreams must never be so important to you that other people become only fodder to feed them. Many of Adolf Hitler's dreams were worthy and idealistic. Still, he is justly thought of as the quintessence of evil because he saw the world as a lump of clay to be sculpted in his own pro-Aryan image. His dreams did not allow the greatest possible freedom for others to pursue their own dreams. We each have a right to dream! The world belongs to all.

Second, your dreams must also hold a certain realistic hope of becoming reality. It is not reasonable for an amputee to dream of becoming a great miler. Old women should not dream of winning Olympic medals for figure skating. I remember a certain friend who dreamed of becoming a Hollywood star. He seemed to me to be limited in talent and drive. Still, he went to Hollywood right after college; he has never to my knowledge ever acted (even in a minor role) in any movie. His dream of becoming a great star was not a totally reasonable dream.

As a third quality, your dreams must be "outline-able." I have a friend who tags himself an entrepreneur and has some gifts in that area. His various ventures, however, are only bridge supports and nothing more. The gulf between where he is and where he would like to be is never bridged by discipline and effort. He is all dream—only dream. Your ability to outline your dreams tells you if the span between your ideas and their realization is possible.

A fourth quality of valid dreams is that they take root in deeper soil than yourself. God is the only soil in which to root a worthy dream. This great God who holds the secret blueprints of life has the very hairs of your head numbered. Nothing of life escapes Him. As an Indian poet once said: "The subtle anklets that ring on the feet of an insect when it moves are heard of Him."[7]

Evangelical Christians have popularized a great truth: "God loves you and has a wonderful plan for your life." The implication of this truth is that your life has meaning to God and must be lived according to a higher plan than your own. Any dream that springs from God and takes root in your own mind is unstoppable. Such dreams become a joyful compulsion! You, the dreamer, then become the very laughter of God!

So great can be the product of your visions that the world will be astounded! You yourself should not be astounded, for you should expect as much. You need not stop and celebrate your achievements. That's a celebration best left to others. You will be better liked when you remain somewhat blind to the greatness of your own deeds. It is best when you are an actor in a performance mightier than yourself and so exist for reasons greater than you suspect.

It is no cop-out to say that you ought to operate by a design higher than your own. Yet you must not see yourself as uninvolved. You must dream with anticipation! Recall the words of George Eliot concerning Stradivari, the violin maker? "God could not make Antonio Stradivari's violins without Antonio."[8]

I have a missionary friend who wants to build a school for Christ in Ecuador. I have little doubt that his dream will someday come to be. First of all, his dream is drawn from that God who has a wonderful plan for his life. Second, he has picked a reasonable dream. Third, he has mentally charted the steps between his dream and its fulfillment. Fourth, his dream not only does not infringe on anyone else's freedom, but becomes a joyous hope for all it touches to foster dreams of their own. His vision is a wide-awake probability, shuttered to his very eyelids. It is as certain as daylight and the passing of time.

Conclusion: You Are a Meaningful Maker

You have seen that you are made in the image of God. God is your Creator! Who can deny that your Maker made you to be a creator too? Whether you create things, ideas, relationships, scholarships, ideals, or concepts, you, like the God who fashioned you, are a maker.

"Let there be light!" cried God as He fashioned the universe.

You can make nothing so impressive as the cosmos. Still, with everything that ventures from your imagination and being, you can discover who you are, and can cry, "I have been made by God, but I, too, am a maker! Here is what I make—see, it is good! What I make cries, 'Let there be me!' As sure as the created universe is the photo of God, this which I create is the photo of myself. My self-image is born in the view God holds of me. The more I see myself as a producer, the more I will see myself as significant."

2

The Imperative Tension: Self-Denial- Self-Esteem

There is nothing so weak, for working purposes, as this enormous importance attached to immediate victory. There is nothing that fails like success.

G. K. Chesterton

Strong people make as many and as ghastly mistakes as weak people. The difference is that strong people admit them, laugh at them, learn from them. That is how they become strong.

Richard J. Needham

My name is Martha Bowers Taft. My great-grandfather was President of the United States. My grandfather was United States senator. My daddy is ambassador to Ireland. And I am a Brownie.

Martha Taft

Many Christians see all talk of self-esteem as egoistic fluff. To them, seeking for self-esteem is seeking to replace the centrality of Jesus Christ with our own self-importance. These teach that the Christian is called upon to abandon selfish thinking and follow Jesus Christ in self-denial. All talk of self-esteem is but a bath in narcissism, they say.

On the other hand, many Christians think that the subject of self-denial distorts the Christian message. Weary sermons on self-denial make life in Christ drab and morose. A continual emphasis on self-denial is a stumbling block to successful Christian living. These "progressive" Christians scoff at such pietistic prayers as "Oh, to be nothing, nothing," because they believe strongly that God wants to make us "something, something." They are shocked at the language of the eighteenth-century hymn writers who spoke of themselves as "worms"; God wants us to be giants, not worms, they say.

So the duel is set. Professional counselors, both Christian and secular, generally say that you can achieve nothing without a generous self-esteem. Many lay Christians, on the other hand (and many pastors too), say that you can achieve nothing of eternal value for Christ without the immolation of ego on the high altar of self-denial.

How can we ever reckon with such an impasse?

The general import of this book is to point out the importance of discipline and product as the key to self-esteem. The idea has been treated by some before me. Psychologists such as Rollo May have developed the relationship of art to the self-esteem of the artist, for instance.

But I would like to press the idea a step further. The conflict between self-esteem and self-denial can only find its resolution in the product that comes from our lives.

When self-esteem billows in our lives, it can become mere egotism. But the opposite is also true. If we pursue self-denial, we face the same inflation as a self-denialist. We may think of ourselves as mere worms in the sight of the great God, and thus may make our own littleness the big thing in life. It is possible to exalt the worm we feel we are until it is giantesque and noble in our eyes. At such a point, we will be as guilty of self-concern as the most ardent egotist.

Jesus called product "fruit" (Matthew 7), which is the expectation of the vinedresser (John 15). Christians—self-effacing or not—are supposed to produce (or "to bear fruit"—if you insist on the biblical term). The Christian's product is a constant theme of Scripture.

Of course, I am not suggesting that product or fruit or good works wins eternal salvation for you. The Bible is quite clear; salvation is the gift of God. The Apostle Paul emphasizes that salvation is "not of works" (Ephesians 2:9), but he also continues by saying that even as you are God's workmanship—His product, if you will—so it is God's intention that you in turn should develop a product.

"Be ye doers . . . not hearers only" (James 1:22 KJV), cries James, the brother of Christ. There is an almost militant sense in which the Christian is to claim geography and converts (Matthew 28:18–20). You are thus called to make, to serve, to do. Out of Christ's commission is born your sense of obeying God, and therefore being special to God; as you produce, your product wins you the esteem of God, and thus you can esteem your own life as well. Would it not be wrong to despise what God esteems?

With similar logic, the secular positivist teaches that to think well of yourself there must also be a sense of product, the creation of something—tangible or philosophic, relational or ideal. As others esteem your product, they esteem you, the producer, and thus you the producer will think well of yourself. In either case, self-esteem grows because God or those beyond you esteem you.

Perhaps the devout and the positivist are not altogether as different as we thought.

This, of course, says only that their needs are not different. The truth is, of course, that their view of God and others may remain quite different. For the man who denies himself to serve God sees himself in a different way than the man who produces with no god but himself in mind. Similarly the self-denier will not see other people as the stepping-stones to his self-esteem, but will celebrate others because of their own unique potential to God.

While the self-denier and the self-esteemer must remain distinctly different, the issue of product is important to both.

There are other possible points of resolution too. Let us examine five of them.

The Theological Resolution

The image of God is the best beginning point in seeking to harmonize self-denial and self-esteem. When we talk about the image of God, we are discussing such things as goodness, holiness, righteousness, and knowledge (self-knowledge as well as God-knowledge). Beneficence, altruism, ministry, kindness, love, forgiveness: These are the dominant characteristics of goodness. The fruit of the Spirit spelled out in Galatians 5 (love, joy, peace, and so forth) are aspects of the image of God that the Holy Spirit wants to produce within us.

But is the image of God only seen in Christians? No, all men have been created in the divine image.

Are tyrants, rapists, and rippers also bearers of the image? Certainly many Godlike qualities seem to be missing in them since the image of God has been smashed by evil. But it has not been destroyed. While real evidence of the image of God may be hard to find, it is there.

Positivists have perhaps given us a great reason to think well of ourselves in their oft-heard cliché, "God made me and God don't make no junk." Can the God-don't-make-no-junk cliché pull us all the way to self-esteem and leave us convinced of our own great worth?

The great flaw of this cliché is that in the libertine, the hedonist, or the Machiavellian, it looks as if God got close to making junk. The truth is that God did not make these "junky" types. The Bible says that human sin wreaks havoc with God's good creation. Tyrants and rapists are not that at birth. But in their lives they have acted against this fundamental goodness that theologians call the image of God.

The secular self-esteemer takes the image of God for granted. His good qualities are seen as natural reasons to feel good about himself.

On the other hand, the self-denier sees his innate goodness as a part of "the debt" he owes God. His goodness is clear evidence that God is gracious to all humans, among whom even the selfless stands as undeserving. This "grace" motivates the self-sacrificing to greater levels of denial.

Self-denial in our own lives must beware extremes. We may make such a practice of denying ourselves good things that we begin to feel as if any enjoyment of life is wrong. At this point, asceticism can set in.

Asceticism is the final deadlock where self-denial becomes stubborn. At this point, we can actually prize austerity for its own sake rather than the real goal of self-denial—our relationship with God. Our blissful denials will make us remote and less understood. An ascetic is often seen as a frowner who frowns because he suspects that someone somewhere in the world may be having a good time. To the more flamboyant self-esteemers it seems that the ascetic is one who pictures a stern and sober Jehovah, leaning out over a gray windowsill in a gray heaven and crying earthward, "Is anybody down there having a good time?" When the joyous self-esteemer shouts back, "Oh, yes," the morose God of self-denial barks back, "Well, cut it out!"

To the ascetic, the verse in Paul's first Epistle to Timothy, ". . . God, who richly provides us with everything for our enjoyment" (1 Timothy 6:17 NIV) must surely be a scribal error.

Is innate joy a part of the image of God? Judging from the strong self-affirmation statements of God in Genesis 1, it must be. God seems to congratulate himself at the end of each creative day. God's satisfaction with Himself gives rise to joy.

In a similar way, joy will erupt more spontaneously from our lives if we think well of ourselves than it will if our self-denial has become a measured and gray way of life. Self-esteem does service to real joy. No matter the obstacle, it finds a way to praise, out of the confidence that we are created

33

by the great Creator, who really doesn't make any junk. Our self-denial will only become a special offering of our lives to God when we see our lives as special. Then we, ourselves, will be wonderful gifts—indeed, the most valuable gifts we could give God.

The Psychological Resolution

By the time you are old enough to choose to become a Christian, you have already been influenced by several psychological factors. It is just as true that by the time you are old enough to choose self-esteem or self-denial as a life-style, how you choose has already been determined.

Alexis de Tocqueville once wrote that in the cradle the entire man can be seen. As we "watch the infant in his mother's arms, we must see the first images that the external world casts upon the dark mirror of his mind, the first occurrences that he witnesses; we must hear the first words which awaken the sleeping powers of thought, and stand by his earliest efforts if we would understand the prejudices, the habits, and the passions which will later rule his life."[1]

Such a proposition does not deny you the right to choose your demeanor; it merely states that by the time of your choosing you are not altogether free in the choice. You have been conditioned by your environment to choose in prescribed ways.

How much you esteem yourself has already been conditioned by how much you have been esteemed. How you were perceived in early childhood determines how you esteem yourself. If you have had a relatively "normal" childhood, you felt loved and esteemed by your parents.

But, as you approached and continued through adolescence, you felt twinges of inferiority from time to time. According to Alfred Adler, you compensated for these erratic attacks of inferiority by trying to achieve a sense of self-worth. You were spurred on in your attempt to think well of yourself by the esteem of others, and if those "others" were those whom you really admired, your self-esteem was given an additional boost.

Abraham Maslow taught that unless you are pathological you have a double need—esteem from others and self-esteem. William James, the originator of psychological pragmatism, taught that success and pretension are the components of self-esteem. Success, of course, is a tangible, measurable component. What you succeed at may often be recorded and sometimes photographed. It comes close to what I am calling product in this book. Pretension is the image you hold of yourself between achievements. It is usually imaginary, but not wholly so. It is based on your successes and then stored romantically in your mind as your "good self."

But your self-esteem ever goes through trials and triumphs. At seasons of success, your inner pretense seems stable and worthy. But at times of failure, it seems ignoble or even contemptible. If failure comes too thickly, your spurious and crudely built inner image may crumble altogether. Too many failures in a row may cause you to see yourself as a mere worm. Personal failure and worm theology may be frequent bedfellows. Viewing yourself as a worm does not come from a healthy sense of self-esteem, surrendered to God in loving denial. Worm theology, I suspect, most often has its roots in multiple defeats that keep us from ever arriving at a healthy and positive view of ourselves. It is, then, only a sick self-denial arising from a sick psychology of self-contempt.

I cannot agree with all that William James and later psychologists teach about conversionism. James saw religious conversion as bad because of its negative influence on your own great need to find self-esteem. Still, much of what they said is true. In your own coming to Christ you were likely confronted with the greatness of God and your own sinful unworthiness. You bowed low at the cross, acknowledging that you could do nothing to accomplish your salvation, that your sin had estranged you from God, but that Jesus had paid it all. So far, so good. But as you rose up you may have continued to consider your "self" as failure ridden and ineffective. You may have had the feeling, "When God created me, He created junk."

I must confess that during my adolescence, the negative teaching of my church left its mark upon me. My sense of sinfulness in those years grew out of all proportion to my sense of self-worth.

The next step for many Christians in their quest to develop self-esteem is to find balance. But in the search for balance they become almost schizoid. They may try to cleave into two halves—Jekyll and Hyde fashion—and their "better half" will practice self-denial while they spend the rest of their years on earth in contempt of their "worst half," which is secretly proud and openly humble. This schizophrenic cleavage earns them the reputation of "self-denial" in the church, but the exact opposite may be true. Their entire reputation may be based on artificial humility.

Self-denial is a virtue only when it is truly sacrificial. When Jesus calls you (Luke 9:23) to take up your cross and follow Him, He is calling you to deny the success you might or do have. This is real denial, and it is immensely different from the pretense which says, "Since I am a failure anyway, I will deny myself." Such a self-conceived failure has sacrificed nothing of substance.

I am not writing this to be harsh with those who overemphasize self-denial. I am merely calling for honesty. Self-denial is beautiful when something of real value is sacrificed, but the mere abdication of a contemptible life is not the kind of self-denial Jesus was speaking about.

In a healthy self-denial there remains a healthy self-esteem. Jesus on the cross is clearly aware of His greatness. At His trial, He does not act humble; He is humble. Nor does He pretend power before Pilate; He has power (John 19:10, 11). Yet throughout His life He practiced self-denial. At the beginning of His ministry, after a six-week fast, He refused to create even a little bread in His own self-interest. And at the end of His earthly life he submitted in Gethsemane to the "cup his Father had given him to drink" (*see* Matthew 26:42). Are we ever to understand that Jesus denied Himself because

He didn't like Himself? Of course not! Jesus did not love Himself inordinately, but He knew who He was and was convinced in His heart that it was right and good to be who He was.

And what about His own sense of success? How did He feel about the product that had issued from His life? I am convinced He is surveying His life product in the statement: "I have brought you glory on earth by completing the work you gave me to do. And now, Father, glorify me . . . (John 17:4, 5 NIV). Jesus was not arrogantly stating that He had done something beautiful, but He knew He had fulfilled what He came to do. This idea is magnificently concluded on the cross when He cries, "It is finished!" (John 19:30). What was finished? Human redemption! The very reason for which He came.

Therefore, continue with Jesus as your model. It is not only possible to practice self-denial and self-esteem at the same time; such a practice is a must if you want to walk in the way of Christ.

The Mental Health Resolution

At times you may need to stop and ask yourself, "Is my self-denial a flight from responsibility or an ego-protective withdrawal?" Your self-denial may not be as noble as it seems.

I do not want to disparage those who remove themselves from the hassles of contemporary life to devote their lives to contemplation, prayer, and ministry. Malcolm Muggeridge discovered a strong sense of prayer and immense peace and power among the monks at Nunraw, Scotland. I have two or three friends who are monks, and I also have friends who are brothers in Christ as well as brothers to each other in an order of the Roman Catholic church.

Still, I have known those who have used the church as a flight from the rigors of living in the cold, cruel world. Religion very often gets sick. In one of his books Peter Kreeft speaks of the "Three Christs of Ypsilanti, Michigan." Three deluded beings in that town each thought he was Christ. Of course, they aren't the only ones. Hundreds of others in mental hospitals around the world have the same delusion.

This is a kind of self-esteem, but it is not healthy. The Greek word *holos* means "healthy or whole." Self-esteem is valuable only when it comes within the context of mental health. Scott Peck defines mental health as the unswerving commitment to reality at all costs.

I do not know how often self-esteem results in mental illness. But I do know that, far more often, excessive self-denial results in mental illness. The self-denier who abandons his world is much more prone to mental illness than the self-esteemer who enjoys his world.

In history the famous ascetic Simeon Stylites sat for years on a pole, separated from the sinful world around him. Others moved to caves or mountaintops. Others had their tongues torn out so they could not violate their own codes of silence. Origen had himself castrated to devote himself to a celibacy that knew no temptation. On and on go two thousand years of such tales.

Unless there is a strong commitment to reality, neither self-denial nor self-esteem are worthy of commendation.

The fact of the matter is that if you want to live a noble life, you must achieve a balance between self-esteem and self-denial. If you hit either of these values too hard, your life cannot be whole. When self-esteem is all there is, life is marked by delusion and indulgence. When self-denial comes without self-esteem, the issue is often one of inferiority at best and psychopathy at worst. It may be a piously phrased inferiority—but it is inferiority even if it cries out, "I am nothing, nothing—only a worm before the majesty of God." Psychopathic inferiority cries out, "I am a worm, you are a worm—let's smash up both ourselves and the whole wormy world around us."

The deciding factor in your balance is your sense of product. May you be able to say, "See, in spite of my weakness, my life is producing a great thing. God has put me in the world, in this place, at this time, for a purpose. Though I may not be developing my product perfectly, I am doing it well enough to celebrate its presence in the world."

You will then find that you cannot celebrate what you produce without celebrating yourself.

The Relational Resolution

Both your self-esteem and self-denial must live within the matrix of society. Others become the mirrors to your self. Sociology, therefore, is your great examiner. You will be able to tell when your denial or esteem is becoming excessive just by watching your acceptance in the world.

Just as psychology influences you in a thousand ways before you become a Christian (and are able to opt for self-denial), so does sociology. If you have healthy levels of self-esteem or self-denial, you will find yourself being accepted as a healthy individual in your world.

The world is your place! When told the world was coming to an end, Mark Twain is reported to have said, "Good! We can get along without it." Of course he could not. Neither can you. Whether you esteem or deny yourself, your esteem or denial must live itself out in the world from which you cannot separate yourself.

When Christ enters the lives of new converts, there is a changing of worlds. The new convert enters the world of church life and often abdicates the larger world where he once lived and worked. Soon his new self-contained world becomes a substitute for the "real" world he turned his back on when he turned his face toward Christ.

Your childhood, like mine, may have been spent in a very rigid church where you were taught that you were to be separate from the world and all its evil, antichrist, and pernicious influences. But you cannot separate yourself from the world! You cannot escape your togetherness with all that is.

Your involvement in the world is Christ's command, but it is even more than that. It is imperative to making Christian teaching and morality felt to the very roots of society.

When Jesus said to go into all the world, He was merely speaking geographically. Sociologically you cannot go into your world; you are already in it. It is your permanent and only possible address. And you must not see the church as a monastery from which you tentatively and spasmodically enter the world.

The world can be brutal and chip at your self-esteem. With secular snobbery, it may mock your genuine self-denial. Still, it is your home. George Washington Plunkitt preached his doctrine of survival as a Tammany underboss:

> You can't study human nature in books. Books is a hindrance more than anything else. If you have been to college, so much the worse for you. . . . To learn real human nature you have to go among the people, see them and be seen. I know every man, woman and child in the Fifteenth District. . . . I know what they like and what they don't like, what they are strong at and what they are weak in, and I reach them by approachin' at the right side. . . . I don't trouble them with political arguments. I just study human nature and act accordin'.[2]

This sort of challenge is imperative. Out there in the social complexity, you must both esteem and deny yourself. Mao Tse-tung once observed to a Westerner that all human beings are marked by two desires: a desire to be worshipped and a desire to worship.[3] The language may be a little strong, but if you replace the word *worship* with the word *admire*, it is certainly true. Most of us want to be admired by others and we also want to admire those who are worthy.

In the wide, wide world of relationships, people will generally think of you as you present yourself to them. If you present them with a confident and secure demeanor, they will see you in that way. If you present yourself as uncertain and insecure, that will be their perception. The surest way, therefore, to get others to esteem you is to have self-esteem. They will also admire your self-denial as long as it is not too blatant a denial of the world where they must go on living. The world is their only possible address too.

The clear resolution of this dualism may be in saying

healthy self-denial will always be admired. As others admire you, perhaps you can authentically admire yourself. You need to keep in mind your tendency toward sinfulness and hypocrisy so that you avoid pharisaism. To crave esteem for self-denial is, of course, sick. But again, to weld the two into opposite and authentic sides of yourself is to see yourself rightly.

Self-denial, therefore, is never the product you seek. Healthy self-denial is the sacrifice you make to gain time or means to make the product. It is the committed and giving spirit that finally takes no notice of itself at all and thus becomes beautiful. As long as you are conscious of your self-sacrifice, your sacrifice is inauthentic. To see your sacrifices and feel good about them is to fake self-esteem: Such self-esteem is too selfish to be denial. It is only self-denial looking holy while it waits for applause.

The Time and Growth Resolution

The mere process of aging can become a great harmonizer of your incongruities. You will come to see how opposites are not quite so opposite with the mere passing of time. Self-esteem and self-denial seem altogether opposite, but the fleeting years may in the end make them but the bookends of real adjustment.

It is true that your body grows only for about a fourth of your earthly years. Not so with your self. My self did its best growing only after my body had quit growing altogether.

Some psychologists see this as a natural tendency. Maslow's word for it is *self-actualization.* This self-actualizing tendency gives you a more tolerant understanding of other persons.

In the process you also begin to see the interrelatedness of all truth. Of course, Jesus is the redeeming truth that saves, but every truth of this world is the friend of that very God who is your Father and the Father of your Lord.

I am not implying that Jesus is just one category of truth among others. But there is such an interrelatedness among truths that to be really committed to any one of them is to be committed to all of them. To be the enemy of any real truth, however small that truth may be, would be somehow to set yourself against the God who is the Father of all truth.

Self-esteem is a human need. So is self-denial. Both are true and while they need to exist in every human being, they cannot be enemies and both be the truth. Loving yourself and denying yourself are not bipolar truths—there are no bipolar truths. Maturity does not make them one; they are always one. Maturity does enable us to see them as one.

Just how much maturity does it take to reconcile the two? It cannot be measured in years since we all grow at different rates. It must be measured in insight. If you always treasure self-esteem, you may one day see that self-denial is not putting yourself down, but laying aside your agenda to serve a larger truth or need. This kind of denial will engrave your self-esteem with such meaning as can only come from serving something bigger than yourself.

And somewhere along the way, every self-denialist will see that self-esteem is that source of toughness in the human ego that keeps it from being crushed by criticisms of one sort or another. Without a healthy self-esteem, leadership is impossible. If you would be a leader you must believe not only in the cause you lead but in your own competence to do the leading. Bernard Bass says that persons with high self-esteem are "more likely to change others, to lead others, rather than to be changed by others or to conform readily."[4] It is true that "if you want to be great in God's kingdom, you must learn to be the servant of all" (see Matthew 20:26), but servanthood for Christ can be a tough proposition sometimes. You will need the strongest kind of ego-force to get the job done at all.

Most all of the great heroes of Christianity became heroes by doing seemingly impossible feats that required great ego strength. Luther at Worms, Gladys Aylward in China, David Livingstone in Africa, Ernest Gordon in the Valley of the Kwai: All of these are tales of servants with ego-force.

But did not their ego-force come from God? Wouldn't

each of them say, "It was not I who did this great thing, but the Christ who lives within me"? Of course they would have said it. And they were wise and right to give Christ credit for what would appear to most as only ego-force and self-esteem. Still, they knew they were capable and they knew the job could be done by believing that it could be done with them in charge. And they must have slept well after seeing God triumph through their lives. Each of them might have modestly confirmed their courage by saying, "Anybody might have done it; still His victory came through me!"

None of the great saints would have said, "My self-esteem was the enabler," but each of them likely sanctified the ego-force necessary for the job. "God, I'm going to do this and I will present to You as a gift the toughness of soul I must have to get this job done."

Perhaps in the fuller extent of time, the whole issue of self-denial or self-esteem would pale in the older, larger view of life. This seems to have been what happened to Bernard of Clairvaux. He sets forth four stages in the maturity of Christians. Each Christian seems to pass through these stages one at a time till he reaches a more self-actualized view of the world.

The first stage, according to Bernard, is the love of self for self's sake. During this stage, we are still rather infantile in our understanding of who God really is and what He requires of us. The second stage is the love of God for self's sake. In this phase of our maturity we love God, but generally ask from Him those things that are best for us. The third stage is far more purist. During this third stage we love God for God's sake. He becomes the supreme occupation of our worship and desire. It becomes our one goal to glorify God and for no other reason than God must be glorified for His own pleasure.

But Bernard does not stop with stage three. The last stage, stage four, is the love of self for God's sake. In this last step we realize we are no credit to God while we beat and flagellate ourselves like the sect of superstitious penitents in New Mexico. To bandy about our own inferior and lamentable worthlessness does God no real service, for it is His pleasure that we love what He loves—ourselves. And without that divinely imparted ability to love ourselves, we will not conquer many mountains in the name that is so much mightier than our own.

Conclusion

In finality, the difference between whether you have inordinate self-esteem or inordinate self-denial is probably once again related to the product of your life. With a sense of healthy self-denial, you can look at what your life produces and say, "I am making from my life some worthy things. It is good that I am yielded, but it is likewise good for my world that I am in it."

With healthy self-esteem, you will not brag over what you produce, but make it a gift to God. Through self-esteem, you will consider your product to be a very worthy gift.

Your product says with confidence, "God, I give You all I am and all that I produce and it is a gift that I much esteem. It is not so much worthy of You as it is worthy of me."

And if the gift of yourself is a gift you have not despised, your loving Father will not despise it either. For God, as the receiver of your gift, must endorse the proverb that no real gift is ever to be despised.

I am near fifty now, but I well remember the time I first learned this valuable truth. I was a child, perhaps eight years old, being raised in a family of nine by a mother who was so devoted to her little flock she had the courage to raise us after our father had abandoned her without any visible means of support. Money was always short, but I had come upon a dime and a nickel in a day when dimes were made of real silver and nickels, nickel. The two small coins hid in my pocketknife box, worth several of their brassy counterparts in today's coinage.

While they were there they were mine; still, I could not reckon that they should have been mine. It wasn't right that they were mine when my mother worked as a laundress to keep me alive. When she would come through the door at night with her hair wilted from bending over steaming tubs of laundry for twelve hours, something in me began to revolt at those two shiny coins in my pocketknife box. What right did I have to keep them when she daily paid such a sacrifice to make my life secure? I tried to give her the coins but she refused. "My lands, no! Son, they are yours." So on she worked and the little coins grew not to like themselves.

At last I thought of what I would do. I took the coins and walked a mile and a half into the business district of our little town. At the Kress's store I found a beautiful little bowl, or so I reckoned it to be. I bought it and they put it in a little brown sack, which delighted me for I knew it would heighten the surprise. I carried the little bowl home again.

That night when she came through the door, I gave her the brown sack. I will never forget how proud she seemed to be as she opened the sack. I later had children of my own and came to know that all loving parents have a special way of receiving a child's gift, even when the gift may not be quite so special as the child thinks it to be.

Still, it was a time of simple splendor for me. I learned for the first time in my life that self-esteem and self-denial are brothers. And that night as I went to sleep I felt good about myself just in realizing the coins were no longer in my pocketknife box. I was smiling in the darkness—I still do.

3
The
Gift
of
You

Man, you see, walks down a lonely road
between two hospitals—he's born in one and dies in another.
Somewhere down that road he pauses and asks his questions:
Who am I? From where have I come? What am I doing here?
Stephen Brown, *If God Is in Charge*

Ships are ships and not shoes. I am I and you are you. The
I-entity is my identity and the you-entity is your identity, and
we tend to be quite discomfited if our identities become
mixed up or confused.
M. Scott Peck, *The Road Less Traveled*

To grow up
is to find
the small part you are playing
in this extraordinary drama
written by
somebody else.

Madeleine L'Engle

Every self is the gift of God. But it is a gift in the raw—something made and yet still to be made. It is a warm paradox. We are made by God, but the burden of our very being is that we are the makers of ourselves.

You are but once! You have never happened before! You will not ever appear again—anywhere in the human clan. You have proceeded DNA-proof from the creativity of a God who never uses carbon paper. You are fingerprint-different from every other person who has ever lived. Your once-in-human-history individualism is the clothing of your self!

Still, we must proceed with caution! Our individuality, which we will call our "stick-out-ness," is ever in danger of being remade into "blend-in-ness." Individuality, like any garment, can be torn away, worn away, removed, or altered. Usually our uniqueness is altered rather than stripped away. The unique features of our personality are generally rounded, molded, and sawed to make us fit into the world around us.

Is the loss of our individualism all bad? Don't the irresolute, unpleasant corners of our obstinacy need to be trimmed away? It seems so! Our jangling differences must be altered. Our insistence on our rights *above* all must be tempered to become our rights *among* all. Our obstructive demand to drive the center lane must be chiseled narrow so others have some (rightful) room to pass us on the path of life. What are we to do? To give all of our stick-out-ness away destroys our uniqueness. Yet keeping it is always a battle of "us" and "them," for we are forever trimming it off others as they cut it away from us.

How can we resist the world's attempt to change our unique characteristics? How do we keep the world from making us more like "they" are? How, in short, do we save enough of our stick-out-ness to maintain our individuality?

Keeping Your Claws

I will never forget a kitten we acquired as a household pet. "Have him declawed," a friend advised us, "unless, of course, you like shredded upholstery and drapes." We wanted a kitten, but we wanted one who would fit into the comfort of our overstuffed life-style. So, at our friend's advice, we had the kitten declawed. He then *did* fit in . . . our drapes remained nice and so did our couch.

Each fall when the first snows came, however, so did the field mice. Mice terrorize my wife out of all proportion to their size. We baited traps and often at night could hear their padded snapping. I always suspected that Rusty (our declawed cat) felt a strange, unsatisfied desire to do a little mousing. But his natural self had been bridled by the changes we had made in his feet so he could live with our drapes.

In a sense, we advance through life declawing our friends and acquaintances. Thus they fit into our world, and they make similar changes in us so we will fit into theirs. Thus nobody shreds anyone's drapes and our couches are all safe. We all can live together because we, in various ways, remove the danger in relationships.

But in the process of getting socially comfortable with each other, you may allow those around you to strip away the stick-out-ness that makes you unique. Some people have such a desire to please others that they give away too much. Others perhaps retain a jangling uniqueness that refuses to budge in front of any peer pressure.

Occasionally, here and there, comes the "undeclawed." Such a person feels no need to fit smoothly into your world. He menaces and you bolt your life against him! He has within him a horrible fidelity to his own uniqueness—claws and all. And while he often rubs you the wrong way, he has a pristine power in himself that intrigues you. The urge to eliminate him swells about him everywhere, yet the world seems to turn around his unyielding, stubborn uniqueness.

Kirstein wrote of Abraham Lincoln, "The superiority of Lincoln over all other statesmen lies in the limitless dimensions of a conscious self, its capacities and conditions of deployment. . . ."[1] These limitless dimensions of Lincoln bore a magnificent product: the preservation of "one nation under God"! In every area of human achievement, society has been led or changed by individualistic men and women. They retained enough stick-out-ness to shape the world in which they lived. Sameness is not a change agent. It lacks the toughness and discipline to leave any significant product in its wake.

You must define who you are in what you make. You must discover who you are in your relationships with other people. From time to time, you may be tempted to use interpersonal relationships for your own advancement by playing one-up-manship. You can spuriously arrive at self-esteem by consistently comparing yourself with others who do not measure up to you in some area of achievement. The deficiencies you find in others will likely have to do with their own stick-out-ness, which can become a possible target for your own snobbery and judgment. Jesus warned us about the hypocrisy of picking motes out of others' eyes while we have beams in our own (Matthew 7:5).

What Will People Think?

For the first few years I spent in the ministry, I so often heard the question, "What will people think?" It was a demon phrase that kept God remote in the heavens and all my judges close at hand. I remember the night I was helping an alcoholic. In a distracted moment, I had taken a bottle from his back pocket and thoughtlessly put it into mine. It remained there till I arrived home. It was late by then and I was bleary eyed. I looked, I am sure, as though there was a direct correlation between the liquor, the lateness of the hour, and my haggard face. So as I took the fifth of "Old Crow" out of my pocket and set it on the dining-room table, it was natural for my wife's eyes to grow large as she asked, "What will people think?"

On a similar night I was called to the Red Garter Lounge to return an inebriated "disciple" to his wife and family. As I walked out the door, my wife said, "Where ya goin', honey?"

"To the Red Garter," I said. Something in me wanted to lie and say, "Prayer meeting."

"The Red Garter! Isn't that a bar?" she asked.

"Yeah," I said, tongue in cheek, "but I will only sit in the Galilee Room and drink Sanka."

"But what will people think?" she asked again.

Early in my ministry I grew a beard. The chairman of the deacons took me out and explained that with the possible exception of Jesus and Moses, beards were always worn by men of low reputation: Hell's Angels, brigands, and the like.

"What about Abraham Lincoln and Father Christmas?" I protested.

"What will people think?" was his clincher. I was able to keep my beard, but not my chairman of the deacons. I knew they could not remain together in the same church. His ready-made answer came from a conscience conditioned by group negativisms and behavior control.

Your Uniqueness Is Your Glory

In a real sense, our product defines ourselves. Was it so important to keep my beard when it was clear that by keeping my beard I would lose a deacon? Still, my beard was not just a part of my appearance, but a factor in how I perceived myself.

In the first chapter we established that our self-perception is tied to our product. It stands to reason, therefore, that we cannot alter that product without altering ourselves. But we can never alter ourselves enough to please everybody. I could not grant the deacon what he demanded merely to keep him as a friend. In this simple conflict, I discovered the ugly tension between stick-out-ness and blend-in-ness.

At the root of this problem is the truth that we all want the maximum number of people to like us with the minimum amount of change. Large manufacturers always seek a product that has the widest possible appeal. Manufacturers determine to present their merchandise in such a way that the largest number of people will use it. A balance must be struck between making a product that does one specific thing and yet has a wide general appeal.

This is the tension of your own selfhood. You want a unique, indelible stamp on all you produce. But you also want to be liked by the greatest number of people. In the drive to keep all your friends, you are tempted to alter what you are until you lose much of your uniqueness.

Our differences celebrate God's reluctance to make us cookie-cutter children. Our diversity is His glory. God could never celebrate sameness the way Henry Ford did in his assembly-line philosophy, "They can have any color car they want, so long as it's black."[2]

Still, you must be completely honest with yourself. Your uniqueness is *not* altered by your friends. They only measure, assess, and critique your shortcomings. You alter yourself to silence their outcries in the hope of making your idiosyncrasies more amenable.

While your life is not a consumer item like Henry Ford's autos, you, like a manufacturer, must be concerned with quality control. Where your stick-out-ness is abrasive, it needs to be confronted and changed. Your excessive selfishness must be trimmed back until you are a person who is charitable toward others who are also struggling to save the best of themselves. Stick-out-ness can be a most unattractive trait of the quantum self. When it lives a life unchecked by the wisdom and sensitivity of the innate self, it can be brutal, even sociopathic.

Balance again is the key. You must make many changes in life without making too many changes. Your individuality is yourself and you must come to the place where you can say, "My uniqueness can stand some surgery here and there, but it is too sacred for amputation. To change what I am on the deepest levels of my selfhood may be to severely damage or destroy the innate self."

We will speak later of Thomas Harris's phrase, "I'm OK—you're OK." In the meantime, it is enough to say, "I'm OK—*just as I am!* and you're OK—*just as you are!*" *Let's celebrate each other in reasonable ways that do not destroy each other.*

To be liked is too great a price to pay if it makes us concede all of our stick-out-ness. Erich Fromm called those with a great deal of stick-out-ness "authoritarian" and those with very little of it "automatons." One becomes an "automaton" by wanting too much to be liked, thus giving up one's individuality. Automatons do not like the responsibility that goes with being different from the world around them.

American evangelicals are in danger of being people of low self-esteem. It is a small wonder! Group approval strips away key character traits and celebrates only a dull sameness. The question of "What will people in the church think?" becomes all-important to us. It is usually a question of taboo and blessing. If you feel as we do about things, you will be blessed. If you do not, you will be cursed, if only in the silent contempt of our hearts.

Why must the church in every age indict its unique disciples and demand of them this gray sameness? The compassionate Christ quickly dissolves into a furious führer of legalism after a new convert joins the church. His sins, which he was told were buried in the depths of the sea, are dredged up and measured with a cruel yardstick.

The church's sin control often becomes an unbearable yoke. God-given uniqueness passes under the dull blade of religious prohibition. Even in church you can become a carbon disciple with no surviving smudge of individuality. Jesus once admonished us, "Do not give that which is holy unto dogs!" (see Matthew 7:6). I do not know all that Jesus meant, but I like believing He was looking out for individuality.

Most new converts in the church are not so much renovated by Christ as they are overhauled by Christian approval or disapproval. They speak of the "Lordship of Christ," yet they are more controlled by the masses than the Master. In but a little while they move from being controlled by divine command to the neurotic no-no's of the congregation. Made free in Christ, they all too soon become congregational captives.

Robert Frost once wrote, "All men are born free and equal—free at least in their right to be different. Some people want to homogenize society everywhere. I'm against the homogenizers in art, in politics, in every walk of life. I want the cream to rise."[3]

The Loss of Individuality

Individuality is at the very center of all that God created you to be! Is it possible that you could have lost it, and if so, how? If it is lost, you may be sure it did not happen all at once. Most likely, the loss of your self gradually began in the wee small hours of some long-gone morning. The incident is fuzzy, but it likely occurred when you weighed just over twelve pounds and were five months old. You awoke at 2:15 A.M. with an awful sense of foreboding. You were generally well fed and your last feeding was in a sweet state of digestion. But like an infant existentialist you were filled with *angst*, that dread feeling that something terrible was wrong.

Out of your dread you screamed into the night. And they came and scooped you up. On you howled. In the midst of their frantic attempt to meet your needs, they made an indelible comment. It was the first time you heard it, but you knew it would not be the last: "Why can't you be like other babies and sleep?" And while you have forgotten it now, you compromised! You stopped howling and drifted off to sleep! It was perhaps a big mistake. You should have screamed your head off and cried, "I have no intention of being like other babies." You should have chomped down into your teething ring and stiffened for the resistance. But you sold out, gave in, and drifted off to sleep. And thus at an age you cannot remember you silently agreed to be like other babies.

Perhaps the next grave crisis of conformity may have occurred your first day of school. It was raining and you wore your galoshes. Remember them? Your galoshes had to be black, of course, with four metal snap-hooks. Why could some creative designer not come up with a three-hook or a two-hook number? No, always it was four hooks.

They stuffed you into a brown desk and called the roll by alphabet, starting with Karl Adams and working their way through to Billie Young. No *z*'s? Would not it have been lovely to have had a Zebra? But no, it was strictly Adams to Young. Bit by bit, some of your individuality began ebbing off into rosters and alphabetical listings.

Everything grew worse in high school: jeans, polo shirts, gum chewing, and marble rolling in study halls. There you majored in the practiced cool—the campus front—the Coors sweatshirt—the constant hiding underneath a brick face. Secretly you enjoyed literature, but you could never be "creep" enough to let on. It was considered "weird" to enjoy Latin openly.

From this point on, nothing can be said that is capable of real objectivity. Paranoia is king! When you look over your shoulder in the class, your peers are out to manipulate you and convert you to something that they feel would be more ideal for them, which is, by odd coincidence, more like them. The professor in front of the class would change you to be more ideally like him too. Over the breakfast table, if you have been married less than twenty-five years, your mate is out to recreate you—something more pleasant and suitable to his or her view of all you might be.

Even people whom I remotely know seem to be after me. The clothing salesman says, "You do not want this. You don't look good in it." (It's the only suit in the whole store I will consider.) A horn-rimmed, snippety young woman on the plane says, "You cannot be serious about your views. . . ." (I wish I had sat somewhere else.) When I encounter any threat to my inner being, I know that I must not surrender that part of my uniqueness or I will have given up the best part of myself. It is inside myself that I am most who I am. There resides the real "me-ness" of life. In one of my children's books I wrote this defiant poem:

> I'm me, and my "I-ness" is special to me.
> Minus my "I-ness" I'd just be like you,
> And you'd be like me and that's nothing new.
> "You-ness" looks good, but only on you.
> 'Cause "you-ness" won't fit where "I-ness" should be.
> My "I-ness" looks great, but only on me.[4]

We must be sure that we do not allow any self-righteous critics to tamper with this God-given inwardness.

DNA and the Spirit

We who follow the "successful" Christ in a day when Christianity is "succeeding" hear so much of the gifts of the Spirit that we are prone to forget that we receive God's genetic gifts before we receive His spiritual gifts. These DNA gifts are the gifts of life, of sound biology and sound mentality, which some are all too prone to rush by to celebrate the gifts of the Spirit.

It is inconsistent logically! You have only to look at the Apostle Paul to tell that he had great gifts. His "spiritual" gifts were those of apostle, exhorter, and administrator (see 1 Corinthians 12:28ff). But you would have to admit that those gifts were there in embryo at least before he received either Christ or his spiritual gifts. It is easy for me to believe that, coupled with his drive, these natural gifts would have made Paul a success even if he had remained a Jew and a Pharisee. But those natural gifts, fortified with the inward power of the Spirit of God, allowed him to turn the world upside down (Acts 17:6).

To understand all you are, go ahead and affirm the gifts of the Spirit, but then move on to speak of your prior gift, the initial gift, the priceless gift of your individuality! The gift of forty-six turgid chromosomes, splitting longitudinally. Splitting and splitting and splitting until every cell of your body is filled with them; these multimillions of chromosomes cry out at once that you are you—and that it is worth the trip!

Further, you never have to apologize for who you are, but you do have to defend it. You have to fight for it! And if you do not, you will lose it. It is difficult to find a single passage for a proof text from Scripture. But the Scriptures are replete with examples of what I am talking about. The Bible is the account of all that God was able to accomplish combining His power with human individuality.

Moses, waving his grubby stick in the face of Pharaoh.

Jeremiah, crying over the destruction of his people.

Isaiah, writing his poetry of deliverance.

Esther, alone, thwarting racism and genocide.

John the Baptist, running his fingers beneath the bark of a dead tree and pulling out the dark, red honeycomb for his dinner.

So what is this lie of *ego surrender* that is often published by sincere evangelicals?

Let no one tell you that if you would have power with God, you must wipe yourself out and become nothing. Do not believe the lie that teaches you must slay the ego and become nothing, for it is from nothing that God creates. "Remember," they say, "it is *Creatio ex nihilo!*" "They" never seem to see the illogic of what they are saying. To create again implies the Father did not do it well the first time. God is good! Not only good, but the perfect Creator, and if He were to ask us to annihilate ourselves, He would violate His own definition. *Abaddon* is the name that must be given to Lucifer, the *destroyer.* But God is *Creator.* God is not out seeking to have mankind become an amorphous mass of sameness. He would not be flattered by having us offer unto Him an inert comatose being.

We become Christians, not by the slaughter of our personalities, but by our willingness to be used. To cry "Lord" does not mean that we surrender the gift of individuality, but that we quit using it for ourselves and offer it unto Him.

The Place of Your Ego in Your Faith

I used to have a pastor who felt that to be a good preacher was to live out the cliché "Lord, hide me behind the cross and let others see only Jesus." How foolish was his prayer! The Lord never hid him so well we could see only Christ. We always saw him, gravy spots and all. We always remain visible as we serve. Even if we have a highly anointed message and our unction is functional, they see the spots. If we paint the Nazarene like Rembrandt but have spinach on our tooth, they will see only spinach while their vision of Christ grows dim.

Being "crucified with Christ" (Galatians 2:20) does not mean that your own priceless gift of ego is to be despised. *Ego* has become a dirty word. It doesn't need to be. The word *ego* is a first-person pronoun in Greek. It means "I." "I" is not something we have but something we are. You are indeed to be crucified with Christ, but not so that you may eradicate your uniqueness. Crucifixion does not destroy your identity, it magnifies it. The Savior was never more His own man than when He hung by His hands.

I have often seen my brothers nailed to crosses by the awful crises of the ministry. At such times, they rise to levels of individualism they did not know was there. All of us turn from crosses, yet crosses best test our authenticity. Under great stress our understanding of who we are breaks down. We may distrust or even criticize the product that comes from our lives at these times. As we lose confidence in our product, we may vacillate, no longer sure of who we are.

Dr. Robert Ardrey wrote of a strange restiveness in our souls. We not only question who we are, but we find our very appetites misleading. We are like ". . . a man who is hungry, gets up at night, opens the refrigerator door and doesn't exactly see what he wants because he doesn't know what he wants. He closes the door and goes back to bed."[5] Crises shatter such vagueness! In the hard times we see again the significance of what we make. Our product authenticates our reason to be, even when our being itself becomes burdensome.

Crosses always try to destroy our stick-out-ness. The judgment of the nail drivers is that we ought to be somehow more like them. The crucifiers always say, "You should have been more like us and this would not have happened to you."

Jesus knew who He was. His stick-out-ness was forged in the essence of God and was not ever to be labeled blend-in-ness. Being crucified was not the worst thing that could have happened to Him. The worst thing for us would have been the surrender of His priceless unique role in our salvation. Such a "blend in" Christ would have been saying that He was a lie and that He really didn't matter.

It is the same with us. Our worst admission would be that if I were like you (and you were like me) the world would not suffer loss. I think the universe would have lost if Jesus, in His third stormy year of ministry, had said, "I must try to be more what these Pharisees want in a Messiah."

The Ebbing of Individuality

Individuality is rarely lost all at once. It is traded, bit by bit, until it is gone. Individualism by individualism! You climb to group approval that way. At each rung of the ladder, you will surrender another diamond from the bag of your uniqueness. Finally you reach the apex of acceptance, absolutely bereft.

A good friend said to me some years ago, "I think you will be successful as a pastor; I just wonder what you will be when you are." The statement was hidden then. Now I have seen enough to know how men trade their virtues for position. (Pastor X has made it now, but then it cost him everything. He gave up his doctrine on the equality of man when he sided with a surgeon against a service station owner in the last church split. He gave up his "firm" convictions about racial integration when he opened a private school during a busing program. By the time he accepted the call to the pulpit of First Church, there was little of him left anyway, so he just traded it all with the understanding that he would be receiving a new car every year to use in "the Lord's work.")

Avoiding the Sin of the Nazarenes

Jesus is the perfect model for a nonbargaining uniqueness. We all sell our important ideals more easily to those we most love. He must have craved love and affirmation from those of His old hometown. I have tried to imagine how it was when Jesus went home to Nazareth. I can hear the hometown folks saying, "This skinny little child we did not understand grew up to be a man we do not know. Why can't he be more like us?"

Nazareth is not a city horrible and different! Nazareth is "our town." It is Thornton Wilder's place, full of ordinary people who love the ordinary and turn from all that does not fit in. Jesus did not fit in: He needed to be admonished, corrected, or spurned. His trouble was that He did and saw the unbelievable; His vision and His faith needed to be brought in line with the ordinary and customary. The Nazarenes were trying to do just that. We must all beware the sin of the Nazarenes!

With my own kids I ever fought the tendency of too much control.

When my son was young, I loved the way he lived alone. Tim was a beautiful boy who retained the priceless gift of himself. As a diversion, he often took his BB gun into the yard and shot dandelions. As the seeds scattered, there were more dandelions, so he bought bigger bags of BBs and went on. Occasionally I would spy him reloading in a clump of dandelions, lost in poetic joys.

I was afraid of dogs and one day I arrived home to find Tim sitting on the porch with his arm around the biggest German shepherd I had ever seen. I heard the low rumble in the killer's throat and I was afraid to get out of my car. I listened through the opened window as my poetic, dandelion-shooting son said, "You will have to go now, Baron; Daddy is home."

Such individuality was his own, and I wanted him to keep it. As for myself, I also do not want to lose any more of mine than I must. Like David, if I must meet a giant I would rather do it in my own tunic than someone else's armor.

Long ago I left a church board meeting. It was an awful meeting at which I was alone in my feelings on the issue at hand. The heat grew; the emotion fumed. As I walked out of the church, absolutely everyone on the board was furious with me. One who could be more tolerant than the rest advanced to me, put his arm around me and said, "Pastor, can't you bend a little—just a little?" And then he went on to speak the obvious, "Everybody is mad at you. I sure hope the church does not have to lose you."

And I remember saying to him. "I do not mind so much if the church loses *me; I* just do not want to lose *me.*"

The Three Crucial Questions

There are three crucial questions you must ask and correctly answer if you are going to deal properly with the whole issue of preserving your individuality.

1. Have you identified the source of your individuality in Christ?

This whole question of individuality can best be answered in terms of our conversion to Christ. Both genetic and spiritual gifts comprise our individuality, and every Christian is first made unique, being human, then "remade" (we are prone to say "reborn") in the Spirit of God in a further affirmation of individuality. Make no mistake, both genetic and spiritual gifts are freely given to all who believe. None are passed by. You must not see God as a partial giver who gives to some but ignores most. The gifts enhance each other, having been given by the same Giver. Thus is our uniqueness twice conferred: first by the DNA stamp and then conferred by the coming of the gracious Spirit of God.

2. Have you clearly defined the use that you make of your uniqueness in Christ?

The gifts of God are not given for ornament but for use. To strut like a peacock over your gifts is to view yourself in an ornamental mode only.

When I was young I spent a lot of time on a tractor. I can remember getting a new plow with four shares. No other farmer stopped by to admire or compliment the new plow. Plows were not to be bragged upon. They were for turning earth and making stubborn ground yield to the coming of the

61

seed. To celebrate your uniqueness without using it is a sin against Christian individuality.

3. Have you put the pencil and paper to the whole issue of your uniqueness?

This third question is probably the most important of the three. You need to do a study to record and measure what your gifts are. You can do this through written assessment. Question your better friends as to what they see your gifts to be. Items that show up again and again are likely those gifts that really do constitute your own uniqueness.

But writing your analysis needs also to pertain to the second question. It would be helpful to write down the ways in which you see yourself applying your uniqueness. As you record the way you use both your spiritual and genetic gifts, you will immediately discover the stewardship that you achieve in their use. Writing down your gifts and charting your use of them will give you a clear vision of your individuality and what it means to God, your world, and yourself.

Conclusion

What a mandate is hidden in this glorious prayer: "Thank You, Lord, for *me*, and make me hard to Xerox." So often we are led by behaviorists or therapists to believe that we are only the creation of DNA interacting with our environment. We have been discussing a loftier origin of ourselves. We are from God en route to God. Each different in our conception, we came in time to life in Christ and our uniqueness is further enhanced by the waiting Spirit.

With such double-formed uniqueness, it is not just unwise to let others steal the prize of our individuality. It is in every sense a sin. If our individuality were only the product of environment and early conditioning, then its surrender would only be an issue of sociology or psychology. But if our individuality is from God, then its surrender is a sin against the Giver.

The church is forever drawing the categories of lostness

and foundness. I believe that in these categories individuality comes to life. But what is lostness? Is it just "going-to-hell-ness?" No, much more! Lostness is "going-nowhere-ness!"— no destiny of any sort! The most tragic thing about spiritual lostness is that it is the loss of the key to our selves. Even if we can see the uniqueness of our own individuality, we cannot tell the source or reason for it.

Conversion deals with the deepest definitions of self. Within the heavy walls of our innate selves we meet Christ, and we are able to celebrate the quantum self that issues from it. The celebration is one God Himself must favor.

How I remember that beautiful Oklahoma night forty years ago when I attended a Pentecostal tent revival. At the end of the service I went forward to give my life to Christ. I was half-stumbling in a new childish joy. I was "saved," as they said, and I was excited about it. I now know what I could not have been so certain of at that time. I had not only discovered God; I had, at ten years of age, found the key to myself. My life opened upon a primitive understanding that I was special. A mystery enveloped me. My world, barely a decade old, grew as joy spilled out of my life.

The service ended and I walked home. My mother celebrated her children with no need to strip away what she didn't understand. Whatever she saw in me, I am sure it must have seemed both mysterious and humorous. There she was that night, a practical madonna as she looked out at her Norman Rockwell etching in size-eight overalls.

"Lady," I must have said, "somebody just found your little boy!" It was a discovery worth throwing a party to celebrate, and so we did.

4
The Cinema Leap

 A boy was born 'mid little things,
      Between a little world and sky,
And dreamed not of the cosmic rings
      'Round which the circling planets fly.

He lived in little works and thoughts,
      Where little ventures grow and plod,
And paced and ploughed his little plots,
      And prayed unto his little God.

                          Sam Foss

If we don't change our direction, we're likely to end up where we're headed.

                          Chinese Proverb

We are such stuff as dreams are made of.

                         William Shakespeare

Self-image is the projection of what we may or will be.

Day and night we talk to ourselves in incessant mental pictures. These images, ever changing, survive our days, our decades, our very lifetimes. How do these images form? Who can understand the mystery of psycho-electrochemical impulses that produce mental motion pictures? All you can know is that your days are spent at a constant cerebral cinema whose inner pictures become the directives of your life.

The imagination wields great sway over your future by concocting pictures of yourself as you would one day like to be.

Sometimes these cinema images dwell on themes of wealth and fame. The ego becomes intoxicated with glorious ideas of success or stardom. In *Humboldt's Gift*, Saul Bellow wrote of this intoxication: "I experienced the high voltage of publicity. It was like picking up a dangerous wire, fatal to ordinary folks. It was like the rattlesnakes handled by hillbillies in a state of exaltation."[1] Andy Warhol wrote of the universal desirability of fame. "In the future, everyone will be famous for at least fifteen minutes," he said.[2]

Still, these inner future portraits come in enticing colors. The image of your finished self is often an overwhelming motivator! These future images are powerful and managerial, always shouting at you to meet their demands. Your every life decision must reckon with their force.

But no guiding image is worthy unless it is a moral and spiritual image. The morality of some who are famous is not worthy of our esteem. James MacGregor Burns comments: "Huge throngs parade in Red Square and in the T'ien An Men Square with giant portraits of men who are not giants. The personality cult—a cult of devils as well as heroes—thrives in both East and West."[3] If the image is worthy, the life it foreshadows may be as well.

The Cinema Leap and the Observable Leap

Most of the heroic images which direct your life are not as politically grandiose as those one encounters in Red Square.

They direct in powerful but more subtle ways. See how these images do direct: The tennis hopeful in white Adidas throws his Head racquet into the back of his sports car and vaults over the side of his convertible into the driver's seat. Is he merely jumping? Anyone watching him has the feeling he "jumped before he jumped." The observable leap was performed in the cinema of his mind before he actually leapt.

The movement toward life goals is the unstoppable course that runs between these leaps. The cinema leap fixes the possibility of all future achievement and the actual leap labels the cinema leap as a genuine and sensible motivator. Your future is thus seen, rehearsed, and performed as a vital function of what you have seen yourself to be. There is a real sense that what you will be you are already, at least in embryo. So the cinema leap is not just a career indication. It's a jump into genuine self-understanding.

In the case of the tennis hopeful leaping into his car, how did his formulated jump first occur? Did he ever once ask himself, "How does Jimmy Connors get into his car?" Did he say to himself, "How am I going to do this after the big match at Wimbledon?" Is he not already behaving inwardly as though he had achieved this future view of himself?

Now consider the power of the cinema leap. It is a moving picture that creates a hanging portrait. It is not just a snapshot it creates: It creates an elegant picture resting in a gold gallery on a high and lofty easel at the front of the mind. This portrait has full sway in the tennis player's life, motivating all he does. He never just buys a sports coat; he buys the special coat that the pro of his dreams wears. He does not eat just anything; his diet—wheat germ, raw egg, yogurt, yeast—all were devoured in his mind before he actually ate. His every outer action is first rehearsed in the quiet of his mind. His whole life then becomes a kind of monkey see, monkey do. The magazines he orders, the girls he dates, the restaurants he prefers, the very way he slouches against a wall, are all only the mimicking of his cinema self.

The secondary aspect of the inner image is more than a fixed portrait. It is an oil portrait in progress where the tennis hopeful becomes the artist, daily adding more detail to the portrait. This picture will at last have the best qualities from every tennis pro he has ever studied. His future image is built from the scraps and fancies of his primary heroes—they played tennis, and splendidly. He only allowed himself to say "splendidly" because he knew that was how Roderigo Fitzsimmons, his coach, would have said it. His coach wore white wristbands with a blue fringe because that is what Arthur Ashe would have done. Here and there he has garnered more than enough parts to fashion his inner image.

Which heroes furnished the best scraps and parts of his composite, directing image? His greatest heroes! Frankenstein-like, he stitched the parts together of that self-made star he hopes one day to become. He thus created his future self, which then works at making his finished self.

The directing image of your own life can be a similar tyrant. It can drive you to become the best parts of all those heroes from which you fashion your own composite image. If this image is so powerful, why do not more of us become the superhero of our minds? One reason must be that most dreamers are not able to become all they imagine. Those who do become like their guiding image not only have the ability and the vision, they are marked by immense discipline and dedication.

Replacing the Cinema With Reality

One reason that some do not become all that they imagine is that they do not learn to respond to the inner cinema in concrete ways. It is possible for you to be motivated toward the development of yourself, but your image can remain illusive. Your mental meanderings may then become little more than egoistic daydreaming.

Lee Iacocca says in his autobiography that he learned from Bob McNamara that writing anything down was the first step in making it happen.[4] Many motivators would agree: Too many people fail in life because they are not able to "concretize" their dreams or plans. Not only should you write down what you hope to become, but you should then write down the actual steps that will be required to make your dreams emerge.

How does writing it down help? Writing life plans reinforces and firms up flabby mental images and forces them to define themselves. As an artist, I always see in my mind what I want to paint before I begin the picture. But something wonderful happens when I touch the canvas with the first swatch of color. My hand begins the hard work of making the outer picture match the inner picture. When the picture is actually complete, I am usually not pleased with it since it falls short of the idealized replica I hold in my mind. But as it becomes real it alters, changes, and firms up the mental image that preceded it.

Success is nearly always procedural! Most people hold erroneously to a "surprise view of success." They live as though life is just going to interrupt them with some glorious achievement. They believe "the breaks" will come in their favor.

The breaks! Those sudden, unexpected, or fortuitous circumstances. Are they real or illusive? They are not only illusive, but unlikely as well. The breaks may come at the right time or the right place, but to depend on them is foolish. Little of value can happen without a sense of direction that is strongly imagined and well-charted.

One of my favorite portions of the teachings of Jesus puts the importance of planning this way: "Suppose one of you wants to build a tower. Will he not first sit down and estimate the cost to see if he has enough money to complete it? For if he lays the foundation and is not able to finish it, everyone who sees it will ridicule him, saying, 'This fellow began to build and was not able to finish'" (Luke 14:28–30 NIV).

Remember that a driving life image is related to simplicity. If you can write down what you want to be and there is only one thing that you want to be, your guiding image will remain powerfully clear. The simplicity of wanting only one thing is a powerful motivator.

As a pastor, I must speak a strong word to others with my

calling. Because we see God as our employer, we tend to excuse ourselves from the planning of life. We are prone to give God the credit for our calling and then to describe our oft-aimless lives with the shibboleth of "letting the Lord lead."

But pastors and other ministers are not the only ones who shift the blame for their aimless careers onto God. Many Christians shrug off their responsibility for planning life by saying that they never do a thing unless God is directing them. Many of them wind up doing nothing of value in life and fostering the idea that they did it all at God's direct command.

The cinema of your future self will not just be a lifelong movie if you live in touch with God. God has a plan for your life that ousts fantasy and replaces it with substantial dream. There is a geometric axiom that says the shortest distance between two points is a straight line. God lays rails to destiny and you can avoid aimless trial-and-error trails. When God guides the cinema, He will take the zigzag out of your pilgrimage. The cinema where God runs the projector is the only safe place to view your future.

The Hazards of Intensity

It is imperative that you see God as being in charge of your life goals and that you do not become tyrannical in the abuse of your body or your mind in your drive to achieve them. You must, therefore, always have a sound respect for your physical and emotional limits. Can you drive reasonably toward what you want to accomplish without cracking under the strain? Be careful. To sacrifice every value of life to what you desire to become is a poor trade. Success that prohibits life from being full in every sense is usually unrewarding when you finally achieve it.

There are so many men and women whose achievements are impressive, but in the intensity of their drive for success, they miss the fullness of life. The intensity of their drive leaves them one-dimensional and blind to the wideness of human meaning. The workaholic is one whose addiction to the grind may achieve, but it often isolates him from the rest of his world, which finds his single-minded interests narrow.

The choleric, driven person will soon find himself serving his guiding image with such wholeheartedness, he may actually feel his burden light. But such career enjoyment may be elusive. The spurious joy of his consuming demands may destroy all balance in his life. Movies, picnics, books, nature will all disappear, and while he may not notice that they are missing, his family and friends will. They will likely withdraw or rise against his lopsided life. Their contempt for his lackluster life will say to all, "Here is a man or woman who is one-track—one very uninteresting track."

Hard drivers usually disappoint themselves and sometimes even abandon their career goals because they are not able to keep pace with their self-imposed demands. Never seeing their limitations, they "crash and burn" on the runway of their dreams. Their muscles and nervous system were not able to carry the current of their high-voltage schedule of success.

Just as the body can lag behind in meeting those demands, so can the emotions. Richard Foster encourages us to remember: "In a culture where whirl is king, we must understand our emotional limits. Ulcers, migraines, nervous tension, and a dozen other symptoms mark our psychic overload."[5] We make the calendar squares our prison. In these little squares we spend our lives coping with the cubes. Too often in our drive to do all we can do and be all we can be, we overschedule. Personal peace flees!

As we fight overscheduling, the evaluation of others is altogether valuable. We measure who we are in the social feedback of all who react to us. We read their faces, body language, and words. In this constant flow of feedback, we understand who we are. James Dobson reminds us: "We are not what we think we are . . . We are not even what *others* think we are . . . We are what we *think* others think we are."[6]

Just as overscheduling can be a physical and emotional hazard, inadequate self-understanding can also impede our progress toward the goal our cinema self has set. As a facet of writing down our life goals, we need also to record our unique qualities in the search for such understanding. Once we have compiled the list, we will begin to see that these qualities are worthwhile. We will then be able to conquer feelings of despair. Doubt then cannot manage us. We will be less tempted to give up and quit. One wonders if the television addict, growing fat, snoring under his tent of newspapers night after night, was not the victim of an inner image he never quite defined. His aimlessness derives directly from a poor understanding of himself!

Affirming the Cinema Leap

The cinema leap finds the greatest chance of becoming an actual leap in the continual rehearsal of the will. If this leap toward unfolding reality is rooted in our own competence and the will of God, it cannot help but become so.

Some years ago I worked at a greeting card company. A friend and fellow seminarian also worked there. Sometimes during coffee breaks we would dream about all that the future held for both of us. I wanted to start my own church. He wanted to become a missionary, perhaps even a mission strategist. After many years we met again. He had indeed become a well-known missionary and I had, over twenty years of time, built my own congregation. Both of us would say that God was the gracious motivator and sustainer of all we became. Still, both of us would admit that through all those years, in the gallery of our minds always hung those important pictures of our finished selves.

Images should major on our own uniqueness and not merely mimic someone else's. I remember in my seminary days those who tried to preach with a high falsetto urgency so as to sound like the most popular evangelist of the day. I remember a high school production of *Camelot* in which a whiskerless sophomore was trying too hard to sound like Franco Nero, the macho singer who created Lancelot in the cinema. When this puff-chested youth drew in his stomach to sing, his leotards loosened dangerously. Acting out someone else's life in an attempt to be just like that person is a fraudulent slur on the whole issue of uniqueness.

Still, such examples demonstrate the strong power that inner images hold. The first writers' conference I ever attended was led by a writer I much admired. He encouraged all the conferees to forge a strong inner image by calling themselves by a title that reinforced all they wanted to become. His statement was: "Never say, 'I want to be a writer' or 'I'm going to be a writer someday.' Always say simply, 'I am a writer.' "

Such constant affirmation has a strong bearing on self-image. Constant belittling ourselves has a similar negative effect. James Thurber has a story about a police dog. Ordinarily such dogs are vicious, but according to Thurber, each night when his master came home he would "thwack" the big dog with a rolled-up newspaper, stand just beyond the leash length and say, "If you're a police dog, where's your badge?" After a season of such insults, the feral dog became puppyish.

Still, the cinema leap is more basic than the achievement it inspires, if only because it precedes it. Your mind, if disciplined enough, can control your actions. And you can control the mind. You can, through tough mental discipline, forcibly wrest negative thought habits from your mind. This is the import of Philippians 4:6–8. "Finally, brothers, whatever is true, whatever is noble, whatever is right, whatever is pure . . . whatever is admirable . . . think about such things" (Philippians 4:8 NIV). Once you have made your mind positive, then your act or word becomes positive.

Creativity and Rest

If the guiding image of your life leaves you joyless, your achievement will be doubtful. You must not allow time or a hassled mind-set make your life neurotic. In the beginning chapters of Genesis, the Sabbath is established. The Sabbath is more than a day of the week. The word derives from the Hebrew word *shabath* which means "to rest." Further, then, *shabath* is a principle established in reference to two ideas. At first, the word is used of God who, on the seventh day (seven is an alternate meaning of the word *shabath*), rested. But in God's case the word *shabath* does not imply God rested because He was tired. He is a spirit (*see* John 4:24), and *tired* is a human word that focuses on weary muscles and strained tendons.

Why then did God rest? God rested because His product was adequate. In six days of perfect creativity, there was a complete universe—hence nothing else to do. God saw that it was good (Genesis 1:10, et al)—an art project of immense satisfaction!

Rest is a strong issue in the Creation story. Why is this so? Because God knew that rest is an indomitable need of man. Much can be said of our productivity as it relates to our leisure. Many studies have been done exploring this relationship of Sabbath and product. Creativity issues most directly from the mind at rest.

We must clearly distinguish the noble idea of rest from the sin of laziness. Rest is the break that fuels life and laziness is a way of life. Rest is the creator-energizer. Laziness is the destroyer. Rest is willing and eager to get back to work. Laziness replaces work with indulgence. Rest is a nap. Laziness is a lifetime!

Creativity occurs at the rest levels of brain activity. There are four mind states as far as brain-wave activity is concerned. Zero brain-wave activity is death. Those between one and four cycles per second (Delta waves) indicate a coma; four to seven cycles per second (Theta waves) is unconsciousness. Seven to fourteen is the sleep or rest state; these waves are called Alpha waves. At about fourteen cycles per second (Beta waves), we are in our action-awareness brain state. The faster our brains function (at higher Beta levels) the less creative we are.[7] Rest therefore is the greatest friend imagination has. Rest serves as a product inspector and guarantees quality control.

Rest not only makes us creative, it helps us adjust to the process of aging. *Esquire* magazine has produced a book on

how a man ages. The book contains a huge color plate showing the same man in red underwear at ages twenty, thirty,
forty, fifty, sixty, and seventy. It is a ghastly portrayal of the
inevitable process that claims us all. This process works in-
cessantly against your own life image. Whatever you see as
your finished self, you must reckon with time and gravity.
". . . At about thirty years of age, Mr. Young begins to realize
that everything is gradually turning loose. . . . Most of the
musculature which once rippled across his chest has now
melted and skidded down toward his protruding stomach."[8]
To keep life meaningful when you see your hair going down
the drain and wrinkles chiseling little chasms in your executive portrait requires rest. Rest understands and accepts, even
laughs at the 4-B syndrome—baldness, bifocals, bridges, and
bunions.

Rest is the great rehabilitator. How is it done? The answer
is quite varied. Rest may come in the form of short naps from
which all work gains freshness. Does rest have to be sleep?
Certainly not. Rest is generally not conceived of as the cessation of all activity. It may be the mere breaking from one
form of activity to another. For those sweltering under the
drive of a powerful life image, rest may be a tearing free from
the heavy demands of career goals.

Certain personality types will find it more difficult to rest.
Arriving at the imperative balance of driving and resting is
the key to keeping our humanity. Lee Bickmore, president of
the National Biscuit Company, spoke the truth when he said,
"No man can become a great leader, or a great success, on an
eight-hour day."[9] But the man who begins pushing the eight-
hour day too much blinds himself to adjustment in life. The
image of such joyful hyper-drivers becomes the master and
not the servant.

John White once observed a young cuckoo in a sparrow's
nest. Cuckoos are irresponsible birds that invade nests and
force other birds to raise their young. The fledgling cuckoo
White observed was twice the size of the small sparrows
where the adult cuckoos had laid their foreign eggs. White
watched the obscene drama of the baby cuckoo: "It amazed

me to see what power the cuckoo held to keep the sparrows on the move. His lusty cries could be heard for a quarter of a mile. The sparrows had grown thin and weary in their endless haste to cram food into his insatiable gullet." White goes on to comment, "Self is a cuckoo in the nest of your heart."[10] This monster image of what you want to become may also make you its thin and harried servant.

The syndrome is obvious in others. Once having spotted it, you must beware its deadly influence in yourself. Pope John XXIII was once counseled by a serious cardinal to move faster in solving the world's ills. The pope looked at his friend, considered his hassled and frenzied world, and confessed that even popes have their limitations. Each time the pope was tempted to think he could really solve the world's ills, he was ministered to by a special angel who came to the papal bedroom and said, "Hey there, Johnny boy, don't take yourself so seriously."[11] You must solicit the wisdom of such an angel. Should such an angel not stop by, let your innate self blow the whistle on your overindustrious quantum self. That outer and busy ostentatious self sometimes maintains its showy outwardness because it wants to be the center of admiration at the cost of every other life value.

Still, the innate self can become the quiet gallery where you hang the unpublished hopes you hold for your future. But your future will be as hassled as your present unless you learn to rest.

Inner Hero, Outer Hero

Avoiding the excesses of a bossy self-image, you can then begin to celebrate its positive, if quiet, aspects. Consider the parable of the Persian crown prince who was from birth a hunchback. When he thought of his stalwart and regal father, he became afraid of succession to the monarchy. There was a dark truth hiding in his mind that told him that royal authority and strong edicts could never come from a bent and freakish frame. In lieu of the fear of the coming day, he hung a portrait of himself in the gallery of his mind: The portrait of himself was exactly as he would look if he had no deformity. His Quasimodo self looked inward to a titan self, worthy of the word *royal*. In his mind he was indeed a king.

To fortify his inner image, he hired the royal sculptor to carve him from firm marble, exactly as he would look if there were no deformity. It was life-size and when the sculpture was completed, a strange and wonderful marriage took place. His strong white marble self met and pledged itself to his inner image. Both images towered above him and gazed down upon their twisted, would-be offspring.

Then, this bent prince smiled upward and made them both a promise. One day there would be the three of them. They all would tower as a trinity of kings. In this dream began his transformation! Gazing into the gallery of his mind, each morning he stood with his bent back against the back of his marble self. He tried to throw his shoulders back to meet the erect and mocking marble of the straight, proud statue. It seemed a piteous display, yet he never gave up.

Day after day; year after year he came. One day, in a royal corridor, he overheard a mop-maid say, "The prince is somehow straighter." Her comment fueled his ritual with great desire. And in a decade came the morning he had lived for. Backing up to his strong self, he felt the cold thrill of marble against his own naked shoulders.

There were now three kings. Two of them were made by his great desire of soul. They begged to rule with him, but they had served their purpose. The marble king was beaten into shards, the picture in his mind had become himself, and he slipped the crown of state upon his head.

But there are real-life stories just like this. These are stories, not of men who fashioned their own image, but who came into contact with God and were fashioned into glory. A pharisee once spent himself getting degrees and other credentials. He was proudly religious and could not help but be alarmed by the many around him who were becoming Christians. Certain elect and high officials hired him for "operation extermination," an attempt to eradicate all Christians from the face of the earth. In the process of this attempt, this henchman against Christianity met Jesus Christ on a desert road. The legalist received a new image of himself as a global evangelist—called to declare the Christ he had previously hated. The strength of this new indwelling image was to color his self-view for four decades. There can be little doubt of the nature of the inner image that hung in the gallery of his mind. His name, of course, was Paul.

This is a day when labels are read and esteemed. The Izod alligator is not ripped from articles of clothing where it appears. It is left there as a strong suggestion that the wearer is chic and certainly in touch with the times. The label, however, matches the inner image of the label-conscious man or woman who wears it.

My wife and I were recently traveling in a lane of traffic behind a huge semi-truck. On a steel beam across the back of the truck was a small, exquisitely lettered sign that said "Joe." It was clear that the driver of the truck was so proud of the truck that he had affixed his signature to it.

But flanking this declaration of Joe's ownership were the mud flaps that hid the great, spinning wheels of his "eighteen wheeler." The mud flaps had a certain expensive look, being the best combination of chrome and white rubber. On each of them, however, were chrome nudes, so shapely erotic that they were embarrassingly sensual. A short, red-faced glance was all I could stand as I pulled out into the left lane to pass "Joe." As we passed Joe, I looked up into his cab to see what manner of man he was. What amazed me about Joe was that he had a kind of Harvard air about him. He had a moustache, intellectual wire-rim glasses, and looked as though he might have just finished a monograph on *The Moral Conscience of Teamsters.*

"Joe looks like a professor," I said to my wife, who was still blushing from her back view of his truck.

"Make no mistake," she said, "you can always tell a trucker by his mud flaps."

I smiled.

I wondered about this simple Harvard-type king of the road. While his face said one thing, his mud flaps did tell me a great deal about how he saw himself. "The diesel satyr!" I condemned. I could tell my wife agreed.

What heroes hum in the mental gallery of this Harvard-like trucker? Who can say? We may be sure, however, that Joe's heroes were shaping Joe's mystique.

Ernest Becker warns in his Pulitzer Prize book, *The Denial of Death*, that this is the age of the hero. But heroes are transient and must die. So must hero worshipers, for that matter. Neither heroes nor hero worshipers wish to die.

For heroes, death is easier to bear because their fame, reputation, and product will survive them. This survival of their reputation is their way to deny death, says Becker. Those who cannot be heroes deny death by picking the right heroes to worship. In thus attaching themselves to heroes bigger than themselves, they do indeed deny death, for their littleness and finiteness is swallowed up in bigness.

But what of the hero? Why is it that he thinks such a denial is possible? He thinks so because of his product, which stays alive and in celebration after he is gone. The hero ever hopes to survive himself far into the future. It is bothersome for any of us to imagine the future going on without us.

One powerful trait of our career image is that he wants to be—always to be. He never wants to die. His all-pushing, overproductive creativity pushes him to leave something behind. Through his product he lives on. Rollo May is right when he says, "Creativity is a yearning for immortality. . . . Creativity is not merely the innocent spontaneity of our youth and childhood; it . . . is a passion to live beyond one's death."[12]

But let us take the hero Elvis Presley, who is a cultural hero par excellence. What is the product he left behind? Was it merely records, tapes, and movies? No, it was the aura of his identity. Some will object that I have named this aura as product. In that sense, everyone has product: from the poorest man who leaves only a small family and a few friends to the renowned thinker whose volumes of intellectual concepts survive the centuries. It is obvious, however, that those whose influences are vast leave an aura that serves as a social umbrella to shelter all who will be inspired by it.

The aura of Elvis is the atmosphere of challenge to young entertainers; it is a "spiritual" motivation to the poor in search of some coronation in life. But more than all this, it is a wide worldview that enlarges life.

The heroic reputation of Elvis first of all served him. Each new record, tape, film, poster, concert, and so forth gave him a "death denying" bigness. But also each of those who formed his fan club had something in common with like-minded souls in Seattle, Hamburg, Tokyo. Elvis's sins were minimized. Beneath the umbrella of his glamour, they saw him in a timeless sphere that was not just their own salvation from temporary littleness, but from their own sense of futility, failure, and death.

Conclusion

Product is a deliverer in many aspects. It sets you free to view yourself in terms of the most basic element of self-esteem: dignity. What is given to you in life does not create self-esteem. Every gift is in a sense demeaning.

It is your product which best serves your self-esteem. Product achieved by your own discipline furnishes you with real dignity. It is admired by others as they are able to acquire it as their own. Your own product perhaps has its greatest value when it stirs others to be creators too. The powerful image in the cinema of your mind produces the quantum self—and this self is visible enough to inspire others to produce. Thus self-esteem is ever reborn in your willingness to let your own cinema self become incarnate in your world.

5
Who Are You When You Are Alone?

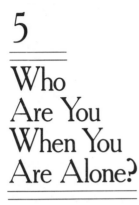 When I went to jail, nearly two years after the cover-up trial, I had a big self-esteem problem. I was a felon, shorn and scorned, clumping around in a ragged old army uniform, doing pick and shovel work out on the desert. I wondered if anyone thought I was worth anything. . . . For years I had been able to sweep most of my shortcomings and failures under the rug and not face them, but during the two long criminal trials, I spent my days listening to prosecutors tell juries what a bad fellow I was. Then at night I'd go back to a hotel room and sit alone thinking about what was happening to me. During that time I began to take stock. . . .

John D. Ehrlichman, *Witness to Power*

A monk was once asked: What do you do there in the monastery? He replied: We fall and get up, fall and get up, fall and get up again.

Tito Colliander, *Way of the Ascetics*

The universe belies you, and your heart
Refutes a hundred times your mind's conceit. . . .
What is the verdict of the vastest mind?
Silence: the book of fate is closed to us.
Man is a stranger to his own research. . . .

Voltaire

Being alone is hard work! Being alone and liking it is impossible for most. Abraham Maslow's third aching universal human need was the need for affection and the feeling of belonging. The world is ours as long as we can feel it is ours. If we have no place to fit in, our misery surfaces and becomes amplified with each rejection of place. Pippin's lament in the musical that bears his name is that cats fit on the windowsill and children in the snow, but he never fit in anywhere. Belongingness is wholeness and joy.

The fear of isolation, on the other hand, is a desperate one. Isolation: that last and final judgment meted out in prisons; the loss of all community; utter silence. But why is isolation such an abhorrent state? Because, as we said earlier, others are the mirrors to ourselves. These mirrors not only tell us we exist, but they reflect our appearance and measure our progress in the world. There are two primary ways we may find out who we are. One of those ways is to see our reflection in our relationships. The other is to seek our unobserved self in moments of solitude. Jesus instructed us to pray by separating ourselves from others and entering the closet. Could it be Christ wanted us to discover something about who we are and what we might become if we could free ourselves from the necessity of always being with other people?

Shutting the closet door behind us is not only necessary for prayer, it is necessary for the finding of character. It is especially necessary to stimulate the flow of creative consciousness.

The Fear of Loneliness

Aloneness is the place of the soul. We can never fully understand the substance of ourselves. But our willingness to spend time with ourselves may not be understood in the current, busy, noisy world. Kierkegaard demonstrated our fear of solitude by referring to American pioneers who used to beat on pots and pans at night to make enough din to keep the wolves away.[1] We often do not like being alone. Indeed, we may be convinced there is a kind of shame in having to do it.

"Beating on the pans" keeps us from having to experience ourselves. Most socially unacceptable behavior is really a heart cry to be liked. Few people ever come right out and say it, but their behavior says loud and clear, "I wish I were more acceptable to me." The misfit is a mass of neurotic wrangling! In a deeper sense than he may be able to understand, he may actually prefer the debilitating state of inferiority since it becomes an excuse for not getting more done in life.

We are often like those legendary beggars who refused to be healed of their blindness since seeing would make them accountable. In a similar way, we often prefer the crowd when we feel socially unacceptable, for solitude confronts us with one great indictment: the lack of product in our lives. Hiding in the crowd can actually become a way to escape the responsibility of producing. We often say, "I'm too busy . . . if I could just find the time to get alone I could produce . . . but, alas, I've too much to do." What a sham this reasoning is! The heart of the issue lies in our desire. Finding an opportunity to get away from the crowd is not our real problem. Our real problem may be liking ourselves enough to want to be alone.

In Jean-Paul Sartre's play *No Exit*, those newly ushered into hell find that all mirrors have been removed. Eternity then becomes for these a loss of self. Perhaps this is the final judgment of hell. It is not just a separation from God, as the theologians say. It is the final separation, even from each other. Sartre did not intend his play to portray eternity, but our own time.

There is a virile loneliness in our day. While we turn from productive solitude, high-speed living forces us to live in microcosms of loneliness and doubt. Were we to find productive solitude, we would see our small product and lament the little meaning of ourselves. We are the nobody generation on the way to nowhere and we are ever alone en route.

More than 60 percent of Americans interviewed by a recent pollster agreed that they were not happy where they now lived. They expressed their ideal home city or state as being somewhere else. This wanderlust must in part explain why one-fifth of Americans move every year. This constant changing of address may well be a continual "beating on the pans." Nothing makes our lives so hectic as changing residences. All the packing and unpacking robs us of any possible time for constructive solitude.

Further, this feeds a cultural narcissism. Each move truncates our relationships and leaves us to face the future alone. It is axiomatic that we turn inward and therefore become ego centered, focusing almost entirely on our own small world. The larger world of social relationships takes second place.

This incessant moving makes us the everywhere people or the nowhere people, depending on your view of our nomadic society. The folderol of change traps us in a constant stream of new relationships. These new and ever shallow acquaintances are sufficient to give us a spurious involvement in a social network. The new suburbs of American cities are mushrooming with suave, rootless, good-time junkies, doubly amputated. They are amputated from themselves by hassled living and from any nurturing friendships by hit-and-run relationships.

Does the I've-got-to-move urge make the restless suburbanite unhappy with his hollow sociability? Hardly. William Whyte suggests that most actually prefer it. Shallow relationships are not so hard to walk away from at the time of the next move. Breaking up close friendships can be emotionally expensive. William Whyte offers us an illustration that serves us well. A certain nursery advertised trees that were easy to transplant because every year they unearthed them and cut back their roots. Likewise, the current suburbanite moves easier with shorter roots.

The Beatles' lament, "Nowhere Man," depicts a man who doesn't have a point of view, makes plans for no one, and doesn't know where he's going. It finishes by asking if he isn't a bit like each of us. The song (which describes our wandering culture) refers not so much to the nothingness of our origin and destiny, but to the fact that between the two, most people do not even have an identifying worldview.

Is it any wonder that suicide is epidemic? When the busyness finally stops, the solitude often becomes not creative but destructive. Suicides are those whose solitude becomes a place for fondling their depression. Most of them have been told, "Get busy," "Find something to do with your hands," "Discover a way to make your life productive." The most likely candidates for suicide, like Sartre, see loneliness as hell that is here and now!

Exactly what does it mean to say life is "hell"? Jesus' favorite term for hell was *Gehenna,* the city trash dump. Trash dumps are those vast acreages of refuse where nothing valuable exists. Hell then becomes God's ash can—the great disposal of life. That smoldering negative solitude cries destructively, "Why am I even alive? What is my life producing that has any real value?" In communion or relationship with others, such questions may never have time to surface. When the parties roar and the bands are playing, we are kept too busy to ask what life means. Weeping, silent midnights force us to reckon with our aimlessness.

One of my favorite writers speaks of what he calls "decidophobia": the fear of making decisions. Decidophobia may not only make us afraid of making decisions, it may compel us into a busy life-style that keeps us running from the necessity of making decisions.

I remember so long ago struggling over what it meant to be "called to preach." The issue was easily put off in crowds, but alone it came to me demanding an answer. No outer counsel seemed to help. I had to decide the issue alone.

Aleksandr Solzhenitsyn said that the toughest form of interrogation was to be stripped naked and forced to defend oneself before a band of accusers. It is a horrible ordeal to imagine—yet at such a moment the sense of our own worth becomes fully manifest. What we are alone before God is what we really are. Solzhenitsyn impresses us as a quiet man, deep as the darkest ocean floor, equally as remote. We have the feeling his "Gulag Solitude" created him in such a wonderful way that no matter how much he tells us of himself, we have not seen very much of him.

Can solitude make you sure of yourself? It seems to, yet you must not forget that the quiet often spawns a loud inner argument that may bring you to the edge of your sanity. In this wrangling silence, you can "yes" and "no" and "maybe" over life in mind-boggling ways.

Could this even be true of Solzhenitsyn? How dare we make such assertions about this noble exile? Because it is the nature of the race. We would like others to believe that once we emerge from our cocoon of silent decision and make decisive statements, we were decisive in the silence. It is rarely so! The silence is only silent to other ears. Our own solitude is raucous and grievous.

John Osborne in his play *Luther* shows Luther emerging from his silent cell at Worms to make his famous reformation declaration: "Here I stand: I can do no other!" It is dramatic and decisive. But at the end of the play, old Staupitz stops by—both of them now old men—and asks Luther if he was really *all that* sure at Worms. Luther tries twice to change the subject, but finally confesses, "No."[2] Solitude makes us real but not always certain.

Aloneness and the Birth of Self

I stated in the opening chapter that your product brings you the affirmation of others which, in turn, brings you esteem. Solitude makes you more productive, but your product can remain well hidden! Solzhenitsyn is evidence that the process is not immediate in all cases. The person who lives and produces in isolation may find his product will not be discovered for years or perhaps ever.

Emily Dickinson was a very productive person all her life and yet she lived and died largely in solitude. In such a case the product becomes all-important, for the celebration of it never comes in time to offer its creator any self-esteem.

Emily Dickinson illustrates not only the important interplay between product and self-esteem, but even more important, how solitude may buttress how we really feel about ourselves. In 1862, Emily sent four of her poems to T.W.

Higginson, who sent them back as unworthy of publication. The setback to her self-esteem must have been traumatic. So far as we know, however, she continued to produce the rest of her poems during the next decade and a half—and these were the final years of her life. Is it possible that the overcoming of this criticism enabled her to believe in what a leading critic had devalued?

It must have weighed a little on T. W. Higginson, who later became the editor of the first four volumes of her work. Alas, it was after her death that he changed his mind. What a boon it would have been to Emily Dickinson's self-esteem had he changed his mind during her lifetime. Somewhere in the extended aloneness that was her life came the confidence that kept her writing. One can imagine the Belle of Amherst celebrating the excellence of what she produced, perhaps not knowing it would be published but knowing it was worthy nonetheless.

Solitude performs this wonderful function: It keeps you from becoming preoccupied with your "usefulness" and allows you to focus on beauty for its own sake. Emily Dickinson may be the demonstration of this principle. Henri Nouwen tells of a certain carpenter who walked with his apprentice through the woods. Passing a beautiful oak tree, the carpenter asked his friend, "Do you know why this tree is so old and stately?"

"No . . . why?" questioned the apprentice.

"Precisely because it is useless," said the carpenter. "If the tree had been considered useful it would have been cut and processed long ago. Since it was only beautiful it stands alone, welcoming the weary to its shade."[3]

In your aloneness you may turn from your productiveness to yourself. In this aloneness you can repair yourself. You are made new so that, going back into the more congested world, you do produce. Even when you do not, the solitude may bring you to the center of your authentic self.

Robert Pirsig's marvelous book, *Zen and the Art of Motorcycle Maintenance*, stunned American booksellers with its soaring success. Who can tell all the reasons it succeeded, but the core of its success must be that it provides a glimpse of the inward self as the point of contact for all that is worthy and worthwhile. This quiet man (with his son clutching his waist), staring over the handlebars at the rising road, does not travel just America. He rides into the center of solitude and in his conspicuous aloneness knocks at the door of all meaning.

Pirsig would say that the premise of my reasoning is false. He would say that meaning does not lie in production, but in our breaking free of the need to produce. Still, the fact that he wrote his book somewhat denies his thesis. His book is his own product, defining what he conceives real product to be. Product is deadly for it seems to take the place of self. Making anything only extends the busyness that keeps us from using the solitude necessary to the understanding of the true nature of things. He would say that man—particularly in the West—is obsessed with himself as too significant. He would see such egotism as the core of our misery. If we can— according to Pirsig—we should disentangle ourselves from the entire material world.

This whole notion is, of course, more Buddhist than Christian, but let us hear Pirsig at least in this amount. The cathexis (emotional entanglement) that you give to the making of things really may create inner strife rather than peace. Your lonely moments then become filled with anxiety over the quantity of your product (are you producing enough?) or the quality of your product (are you really making anything worthwhile with your life?).

To avoid this double bind, you must get God involved in your solitude. Your aloneness may become as neurotic as your need to succeed. The Almighty made you to enjoy Himself and a focus on His presence will keep you from seeing the issue of yourself or what you produce as all-important.

Solitude: Heaven or Hell

Solitude may be heaven or hell, depending on how you use it. If it becomes the province of self-pity or depression, it will be a hell. But if it becomes a time of creating, it will become a point of celebration for yourself and others. There is no end to the examples that aloneness can be productive. Blindness may seal Milton away from some involvement as deafness did Beethoven, but in the resulting solitude their product proclaims their greatness.

I remember so very well a young man who came to my study with grave questions about the value of his life. He confessed to me that in the previous week he had twice contemplated suicide. He was well dressed—spoke with crisp college grammar—he was neat in appearance and had an expensive apartment on the right edge of town. He wanted to be a recognized artist and, while he had a good job, it was no fun.

Complicating this deficiency, his wife was critical of his job and "graciously" helped him rehearse all the failures of his life and career. Because of his wife's criticism, he was in a negative mind-set that caused him not to hear many of the fine affirmations he did get. He really meant it when he said, "My life is hell!"

I tried to show him that his self-erosion was due largely to the negative reinforcement his whipped psyche chose to believe. His continual rehearsal of his faults and failures was literally wiping him out. He was mis-spending his solitude! While God observed his lonely wrangling, He did not condone it.

It is not altogether as simple as it sounds, but there is some truth in saying life is ever what you make of it. There is an Eastern fable about a guru who, chased by a tiger, fell into a pit. He did not perish, because he caught hold of a root growing out in the pit. Hanging there with the tiger roaring above him and the pit gaping beneath him, he saw a leaf protruding from the wall. The leaf was coated with wild honey. He plucked it and licked off the sweetness. The story has some shortcomings, but it contains a vital truth: Whatever your circumstances, heaven is where you construct it.

Victims of depression are not just at the mercy of low self-esteem, they suffer from what I like to call malignant masochism. Scott Peck, in *People of the Lie*, pictures a boy whose evil parents had afflicted him with such an unwanted feeling, he picked sores all over himself in an attempt to get rid of himself.[4] Malignant masochism is an inner urge to pick our selves away until we simply cease to exist.

I have seen this masochism many times. Old people with little reason for living almost seem to will themselves dead rather than face the paralyzing fatigue of living. Shakespeare shows the unrequited love of Romeo and Juliet as diminishing to the point of mutual suicide. The film *The Pawnbroker* shows the masochistic pawnbroker as he impales his own hand in an attempt to hurt with all the suffering humanity who entered his shop.

Usually this malignant masochism is erosion more than explosion. The vacant stare, the manic tears that will not quit. Such crying spells are the dry heaves of hurt. The disconsolate schedule that keeps the alarm clock going, complete with the routine, and yet the overall feeling that nothing is going or at least nothing is going anywhere. Such a mystique wills lonely withdrawal. It is not a nurturing aloneness such as a healthy Christian celebrates in the prayer closet; it is a destructive loneliness that soon sees no reasons to live. Physical death is really beside the point. Death for these occurs before their bodies die. For these, death is a cessation of all meaningful silence.

You must remember that solitude is constructive and loneliness may be destructive. Some solitude may be destructive when it fosters irresponsibility. Some mystics have used prayer as a way of appearing holy when it really became a pretense to keep them from having to live in the real world. When you want to escape the real world, your solitude may be neither productive nor healthy.

Your unwillingness to be alone forces you to live with the truth that you are only the reflection of the crowd with which you travel. A teenager's mother came to me in tears. Her son had been arrested for fraud and possession of drugs. He was a handsome and stalwart lad: not only a good student but congenial in the presence of adults (an admirable quality in youth). However, one item in the mother's attitude troubled me. She placed all the blame for her son's criminal conviction on his associates.

"If I talked to one of the mothers of another of those arrested with your son, do you think she would tell me that your son was lily-white but had been spoiled and corrupted by her son?" I asked.

She thought about the proposition for a moment and said, "I see what you mean. She would likely feel that her wonderful boy had been corrupted by the bad influence of my son." The truth struck her so hard that she broke into tears with the realization that her son might be the "corrupter" as easily as the "corruptee."

Our crowd does define us.

Solitude: The Womb of Character

Back then to the premise of this chapter: Who are we when we are completely alone? The primary issue is character. What a person is all by himself he *really* is.

Living in solitude is camping in the innate self. The quantum outer self retires from its exhibitionism, and the glory he might have brought with him to make us think well of ourselves is absent. Still, aloneness is a friend to the development of the imperative inner self.

Let us consider how character is forged by aloneness. Character is, as the old cliché teaches, more caught than taught. Parental models are doubtless the most overwhelming influences of character. Woodrow Wilson's father was a Presbyterian minister. He, to young Woodrow, was a paragon of success. But if he modeled success well, he did poorly with modeling generosity of spirit. Woodrow's quiet adolescence was lived in fear that his father would be disappointed with his self-perceived incompetence. On one occasion, his father referred disparagingly to his thin, developing moustache at a moment when the manse was full of adults. The insensitive remark drove Woodrow further into himself. Still, we are left to wonder that without this fearful inwardness, would Wilson's life have become a heart cry for the League of Nations? While the League of Nations ended in failure, would the United Nations have come to be without the foundational plea the League made reasonable? Much of Wilson's character may have begun developing in such awful solitude.

Once you reach the level of maturity where your basic character is molded, you must live in the world on your own. But the test of how you behave in your world—your goodness or irreverence—stems from your sense of personal independence from the need of always being in a crowd.

Alan Loy McGinnis speaks of this personal independence as a key ingredient of charisma. He points out that many of the key figures of history appeared eccentric because they spent so much time alone. Carl Sandburg once speculated that most of Lincoln's greatness in history came from his solitary years as an Illinois woodsman.[5]

Harrison Salisbury wrote that Deng Xiaoping, whose much touted reforms of Chinese communism have brought new accessibility to the West, was created by the loneliness of exile. While imprisoned in a tiny courtyard in Northern Giangxi, he would often walk alone, creating in solitude a man who would rule China well when he was more than eighty years old. His daughter, who often observed Deng, said that he would walk alone with his head bowed, allowing his faith in his ideas to become clearer. All the while, of course, he was getting his life ready for the hard battles he must win to renew the life of a dawdling communist state. When Mao finally called him back to the service of China, he said of his old antagonist that "Deng had been forced to suffer every conceivable kind of indignity. Now . . . Deng was like a needle wrapped in cotton—sharp but gentle."[6] Following Mao's death Deng was exiled one more time, and each of these lonely separations forged him all the more into a courageous leader.

It is a mistake to assume that leadership is a matter of being "one of the boys." True leaders are men and women accustomed to loneliness. Their lives are marked at times by near monasticism. Yet from these times of social separateness

they acquire a depth of character that intrigues those less accustomed to voluntary aloneness. Psychologist Nathaniel
Branden says, "Innovators and creators are persons who can
to a higher degree than average accept the condition of
aloneness. They are more willing to follow their own vision
even when it takes them far from the mainland of the human
community. Unexplored spaces do not frighten them—or as
much as they frighten those around them. This is one of the
secrets of their power. That which we call 'genius' has a great
deal to do with courage and daring, a great deal to do with
nerve."[7] It does, initially at least, take courage to seek times
of separation from others: the courage to be different. But
this is true only at first. Once the power gained in solitude is
discovered, it becomes a feasting place for nourishing the
leaders and thinkers of this world.

The problem is that the public side of genius seems to con-
ceal its acquisition. Genius is so appreciated that it leads us to
believe it is born in public demand. It is like the fascination
of the grandstand focused on an Olympic skater. Her excellence belies the discipline of her art. For years she skates in
lonely amphitheaters where all the bleachers are dark and
empty. Only for five minutes is there the roaring crowd. Her
lonely discipline creates her genius. Public congestion briefly
celebrates it.

There might be some question as to whether your character makes for good product or the quality of your product
produces character. Your character will issue from solitude,
however, whether there is any visible product or not. Sometimes in the pain of rejection or ostracism there is a sorting
through of those items and issues that really make the difference in life. It is in this lonely place where you assess if you
are losing; yet losing is winning when you understand that to
lose face or station may be desirable if great principles are
being cherished and their exaltation is the reason for your
apparent losing.

I recently met a young seminarian who was congenial and
bright and one whom I would mark as a mover in the world
of the future. He was engaging in his commitment to God

and the fullness of life. "How did you come across such adjustment, social ease and, above all, such commitment?"

"I was in the navy for a few months," he answered.

"A few months?" I asked.

"I got busted for drugs. I was a bad seaman and caused a lot of trouble aboard ship." He was embarrassed that he had wasted some of his life. "I credit my turnaround in life to sixty days of solitary confinement. From that hellish loneliness that nearly drove me mad I was at last driven sane. I owe everything to my court-martial!"

I remember reading that Solzhenitsyn once said, "Prison, I bless you." Perhaps the young seminarian was blessing his solitude for all the clarity of vision it had afforded him. I think it is a small wonder that from jails came such great works as *The Gulag Archipelago, Pilgrim's Progress,* and half of the New Testament. My young friend himself found God in the agonizing, endless silence of a jail—and only then was he usable to God. Perhaps, like Solzhenitsyn, he will one day look back on a fruitful life and say, "Prison! I bless you!"

Solitude and Self-Esteem

In the lonely inner sanctum of great loss, you can learn what Jesus learned in Gethsemane: It is better to be right than thronged! Gethesemane in Scripture represents that place where despair and victory overlap. Solitude affirms the rightness: The crowd actually cries, "Crucify!"

Surviving Gethsemanes always spells self-esteem. Gethsemane is not the same self-made braggadocio of the man who struggles upward to the bronze award of his own excellence. It is a quiet certitude that says, "I did it. I fought my way through popular fallacies and did the right thing through all my lonely trials."

But Jesus willingly faced the lonely struggle and asked His disciples to remain separate from Him. You cannot take that imperative step into solitude easily. You cannot hope to make Gethsemane a party. You are prone to turn from aloneness even in the heaviness of a crisis.

Solzhenitsyn's Gethsemane may have been the gulag where his novel *Denisovich* was born long before he won the Nobel Prize. Jonas Salk, Einstein, and the Curies all knew how to be alone and to celebrate who they were. Yet, their celebration was not the arm-twisting work of patting their own backs. Their celebration was their work—it held them captive by the sheer weight of its importance. Who they were they derived directly from the product that marked their lives.

Enduring Gethsemane is always lonely work—yet paradoxically you are never alone. In your aloneness you find the glory of your importance to God. And having found this importance, you can never be unimportant to yourself.

Conclusion

There is a paradox at the heart of this chapter! We like being alone only when we like who we are. On the other hand we really cannot learn to like ourselves unless we do spend time alone. If we are terrorized by solitude, we will not be able to use it constructively. A constructive use of aloneness clears away negative thoughts and organizes our inwardness. Character itself is often the gift of aloneness.

The first step toward character is the hard choice to separate ourselves from our busy schedule. The quiet life is amazingly close to the hurried one, yet few take arms against their harried, stifling involvements. Those who do, find in the quiet such treasures as confidence, direction, and self-worth.

In self-willed, sturdy solitude we come to celebrate ourselves and often find that the world around us has seen the reason for our celebration and also applauds.

6

Dealing
with the
Sweepstakes
Delusion

"You seem to have more of everything than anybody else. You have more cars, more televisions, more refrigerators, more of everything. In fact, I've noticed that you also have more books on how to be happy than anybody else."

W. E. Sangster

A husband and wife contributed $2,000 to their church's mission campaign. When the check bounced, they explained with embarrassment that they wrote it by faith, believing God would miraculously add that amount to their account.

Ronald Dunn, *The Faith Crisis*

Men Wanted for Hazardous Journey. Small wages, bitter cold, long months of complete darkness, constant danger, safe return doubtful. Honor and recognition in case of success.

An ad by the polar explorer Sir
Ernest Shackleton and published in
London newspapers in 1900

Will it ever come? The windfall? The Publishing Lottery Finale, when they announce the number and YOU hold the $7 million stub? There seems to be in all of us a sense of some coming inheritance! It is a glorious impending! Tomorrow or the day after, life and fortune will finally meet us at the bank. Ease as we have never known it will be ours. Rich substance will fall upon us. Our car, our house, our future, our wonder, our right to control will move us at last to the proper side of town. Leisure will reign. No more drab routine! No more time clocks! The back-breaking rituals that have held our nose to the grindstone of plain living will leap the rails of boredom. But what is it, in the meantime, that forestalls the event? Why did it not happen today? Didn't we stay up late enough?

Samuel Beckett's *Waiting for Godot* is a long rehearsal of expectancy. Vladimir and Estragon speak all through the play of the one grand event. Godot is coming! All life will be transformed! Heartache will be swallowed up in fullness! Poverty will shed its rags and glory in instant velvet![1]

For Christians, the coming of glory is built into our very theology. We expect Jesus! The Second Coming of Christ will be the glorious finale to this "vale of tears" called life. Jesus ... back again after all those years! It is lottery time—the great historical sweepstakes. Then we shall have streets of gold, gates of pearl, and many crowns.

Waiting for Godot is an earthy parallel of the idea of the Second Coming. *Waiting for Godot* is a universal notion. Someday our needs will be erased by the Midas times of abundance and leisure. Most of us condense the one great answer of life to five letters: M-O-N-E-Y. Money is seen to be the great healer. If only we had enough of it, all our woes would be transformed. Leisure would gild our comfort. Tevye in *Fiddler on the Roof* laments that if he were a rich man he wouldn't have to work, but would still have a great big house. To become rich is the great goal: not merely rich but "easy rider" rich and preferably all at once!

Ignoble Giveaways

To be a literal "sweepstakes" winner would, of course, accomplish this. This sweepstakes mentality exists at the heart of the affluent West. If life can be handled . . . if the breaks come and we seize upon them . . . if we can buy bullishly and sell bearishly, we can stack the lotteries of life in our own favor.

Twice in my life I have become friends with those who won big on television "giveaway" shows. A part of the "take" in both cases was a new car. In each case my friends were as proud as if they had just painted the Mona Lisa. They became as popular in their little world as a rock star. They thought well of themselves and were furiously congratulated by smiling admirers. Why? They were the instant inheritors.

TV giveaways are marked by a nearly ecstatic audience-hype. I discovered Christ in an enthusiastic church that celebrated its joy in nearly athletic worship. But even their unbridled religious ecstasy could never compare to that of television giveaways where people cheer and weep! They whistle and shout as each new round of washers, dryers, and Lemon-Pledge-for-life gifts are ladened upon the joyful receivers.

Those who receive the abundance stand while dollars rain upon them. They say magic words and stuffed ducks belch out of openings with little puffs of smoke. There are even more gifts! Skylarks and dream homes bring cheers and wild stomping. Ocean cruises to Pango-Pango are announced and the bewildered winners giggle and kiss and hop up and down. Lighted panels blink like the control board of the Starship Enterprise as a wild winner embraces a model in a mink coat with such exuberance that they both nearly tumble into a newly won Mercedes convertible!

Have we in the West lost our way in this matter? Does our lust for the instant inheritance not mark us as a people of greed? We seem to have become the people who live only to receive, and living only to receive is somehow set against the meaning that comes from work.

Product and the Meaning of Selfhood

The lust to have lies at the root of the lucky-lottery syndrome. It is not born on television giveaways, but in the very way we have come to regard our occupations. We have become those who work only for the paycheck. The paycheck blinds us to the importance of the forty-plus hours a week we gave to earn it. But as most have come to see it, they are only making money, not product. What is made is drab and daily. The magnificent money comes on the fifteenth and the thirtieth of each month; it is the money and not the making that is treasured.

But what happens when nobody cares what they make? Product control becomes an enforced necessity. Item by sluggish item, the line moves forward: a nut, a wire, a coil, a plastic rivet—each to be added at the proper interval. But the key word is *incentive,* not *quality.* The counting lever must be tripped and the tally recorded so the paycheck will note the influence of the flying fingers—nimble because the fifteenth and thirtieth of the month are coming.

Of what significance then is the modern worker? When you prize nothing you make, do you really make anything? Most do not see themselves as makers, only workers. Most workers do not define themselves in terms of their product, but in terms of the company they serve. If you ask an automobile maker what he does for a living, will he not reply that he works for Chrysler rather than builds Chryslers? Men see themselves as a part of the Honeywell system, rather than builders of superb computers. "I've worked at Norelco for thirteen years" is a more customary answer than, "I make hairdryers."

Guilds, in the Middle Ages, were the forerunners of the unions. In those days, though, the artifact was the definition of the artist! The artisan was a maker. From generation to generation, artist trained apprentice and each apprentice struggled to become an artist. It was not a hurried process. No mason carried stones, but no journeyman could hope to become a mason until he had spent a lot of years carrying stones.

A father passed his calling to his son. Generations of stone-cutters all in one family worked until the great-great-grand-father's descendants finally set the heavy gargoyles atop the cathedral, two hundred feet above the thatched roofs of their village. The artists lived in humble dwellings. Unlike modern producers, they did not labor to constantly change houses, moving up, up, up in the world of elite suburban neighborhoods. One house for a lifetime was enough. One set of good tools and one good stone was enough for each day's work. Leisure came when work was done, but each of them would say it was the work, not the leisure, that told each man he mattered.

What did these simple product-oriented people make?

In the fashioning of stone, their hands grew old in the duties they had chosen. If asked what they did, the artisan would likely answer in terms of greatness. Would a stonecutter have said, "I'm from the guild in Amiens" or "Rheims" or would he have answered, "I'm a mason" or "carpenter"? Not at all! He was building a cathedral and he thought of his whole life in terms of his product, not his task.

While the guilds flourished, the idea of some sudden inheritance was a waste of time for the worker. He would inherit nothing. There were festivals and holidays, but never sweepstakes or giveaways. While the poor had no reasonable hope of inheritance, they knew who they were and found meaning in what they made.

Did these artists ever have a day off? Did they ever enjoy leisure? Leisure was treasured, but it was not seen to be the great good of life. It was certainly not the goal of life. Creativity was the prize! Making something—anything—made life! Renaissance was the anthem of man, the emerging maker of beautiful things. Man was, like God, a creator who could exert force against an encircling dead world and push its crushing coil back as far as his creative powers would allow.

The Renaissance was the frontier of cultural awakening after the long-dead slumber of the Middle Ages. Frontiers always wake the making spirit of man. The idea that men were makers was implicit in the American homestead laws. The land of the unmeasurable West could be had, but not just by claiming it. A person had to live on the land and make it different than when he received it.

I grew up in that section of Oklahoma called the Cherokee Strip. The "Strip" was the land opened up by "the Run of '89." The hardy men and women who gathered up at the state line could, at the sound of a pistol, ride madly into the uncharted territory and claim land as their own by driving a stake into the ground. It was not really a stake they drove, but their lives. Year by year, bending their backs over hand-plows, they produced. The mules that pulled their wagons into the land also pulled their shiny plowshares, gouging the virgin sod.

In my young years, I knew many of these old-timers, and the vigor of their lives had not diminished. They had a "Pearl Buck" romance with "the Good Earth." They had won the right to the romance because of the stake they had driven. The land was theirs! No instant inheritance came! No sweepstakes!

They knew the truth: All life is the gift of discipline.

Rene Dubos discusses life in the Netherlands prior to the building of the Zuider Zee. The dikes were life for they kept out the sea. No open debates or community quarrels were permitted when the sea roared against the dikes. Every man was expected to fight the sea with a shovel. In some areas of the endless levees, a man could have his dead body thrown into the breach to become a part of the dam if he refused to maintain his dike. There was even a law called "dyke and depart" which said that a man who stuck his shovel in the eroding levee and left it to the sea gave his farm to the first man who came along and pulled out the spade and defended the farm by closing the breach in the dike.[2]

All of this was a way of life in the Netherlands. The country was a gift to those who spent their lives dedicated to the propositions that their fortune and toil were married each to the other. An early Russian revolutionary said: "The revolutionary spirit expresses itself not so much in violent methods as in the fact that each single action of every day is related to the whole."[3] It is always those who know how to relate every day to the whole that somehow find meaning in life.

Chiseling the Years From Our Lives

The whole problem with the sweepstakes delusion is that it is deceptive. It separates your days. It presumes that a day is coming different and wealthier than the others. In its anticipation, you may be lured into a darkness that keeps you from seeing or treasuring the present moment. When you quit living in the present moment, you chop off segments of life as worthless. This day does not matter because it is not "the day." Thus, instead of carving time to your standards, you sculpt yourself into the weary pattern of the days. Judith Deem Dupree wrote:

> Brightly, too brightly
> I turned to the wall,
> And cut me a doorway
> Two inches too small.
> Quickly, too quickly,
> I picked up the knife
> And chiseled the inches
> Away from my life.[4]

Jesus was warning you against this tendency when He said, "Take therefore no thought for the morrow: for the morrow shall take thought for the things of itself. Sufficient unto the day is the evil thereof" (Matthew 6:34 KJV). Jesus was telling you never to let your concerns for the insecurity of tomorrow steal your peace. In just such a way, you must not let your excitement for the coming inheritance, glorious as you may envision it, replace your full use of today. The only place you can find life is in the moment. There is nowhere to live but the now! It is true that the career image must be allowed to do its motivating work. But this image must not paralyze the moment, for paralyzed moments do not gather to form a living future. Paralysis and death are frighteningly similar.

How you arrive at meaning is the issue of the present day. If you conceive of leisure as the *summum bonum* of existence, then it, not career, becomes the driving force of your life—your *raison d'etre*. The quest for the good time is perhaps what lies at the bottom of leisure. There are at least three reasons why the leisure drive is unworthy as a motivation to meaning. First, leisure results in boredom. Second, there is a narcotic effect in the pursuit of leisure for its own sake. Finally, the neurotic fear of the loss of leisure is the automatic corollary of too much time on your hands.

It is not just that we have too much time. We do not value time as we hurry toward the future. The future is always where we would like to be, especially in the present moment. And what future is it? It is always the future of Nirvana! Like children at Christmas we can hardly wait for the arrival of our inheritance. I remember the simple wisdom of my mother one Christmas season as I impatiently waited. "I wish it were Christmas!" I cried. "With such wishes you will wish your life away!" she said. Her words were wise!

The hope of leisure and inheritance can make you crave the future. Are you going to be pleased with the future when it arrives? Probably not! The future will probably disappoint you because when it arrives it will likely become only the boring "now." Why boring? Because the future always turns out to be only the same unfulfilling present. The great curse it lays upon us is that we hurry too fast to see or experience the thousand wonderful "nows" through which we blindly pass. It is even as the wag remarked: "I have seen the future; it is very much like the present only longer."

But what about those definite times when the future turns out to be better than the now? Discovering the future often ends with the remark, "I thought it would be better than this." Even if you do win the sweepstakes, you will quickly adjust to your new status and find yourselves disconsolate that it was not more. Being baptized in substance will do nothing to enhance the meaning you anticipated. The most immediate response to winning is: "I have it all, WOW!" The long-range disconsolation: "So what?" In such a response the winner is really saying, "I am now living for the next sweepstakes—perhaps it will be even better!"

The most glorious thing about anticipation is that it seems to relieve boredom. While we wait for Godot, we are happy. As long as we can say, "He is coming!" life seems worth it all. Where there is no "comingness" in life, a hopeless gloom begins to sit in the soul. But when this comingness becomes life, life really never arrives precisely because it is always on the way.

The Leisure Delusion

From this standpoint, retirement is a leisure delusion as disappointing as the sweepstakes delusion. You may prepare for retirement all your life and, suddenly arriving, the leisure you thought you would treasure becomes an encircling coil of boredom. Retirement is the great hypocrite. For years it promises you joy and leaves you at last disconsolate. Retirement is often stifling leisure: It can become aimlessness with no direction. Nothing is here and nothing is coming. You will then have time to go anywhere in a life that is going nowhere—there might be little to fill your time except casket shopping, or some other morose preoccupation with your own finality.

Work can blind you to the sense of its own glory! Work is not just drudgery. It is something you do. It furnishes you with a social context: From work we derive our friends; in work are found our athletic pursuits in union picnics or corporate tennis, bowling, and softball leagues. Work furnishes you with a lifelong dream: the positive dream of becoming the head of your company or at least one of its major powers. While you work you dream of being free of the company.

But is it the dream that furnishes you the best meaning? No! It is the product. You are doing something! What? You are making the chips fly, that's what! Once your job is left behind, you will no longer make anything. The very definition of yourself as a maker begins to change! You are forced to see yourself as a nonproducer. When you do not produce in a productive society, you are dead as a social contributor. A feeling of uselessness then sets in, for the imperative tension between your quantum and your innate selves decays. The quantum self builds its image, to a great deal, around its involvement in the mainstream of life—and, above all, product. Once you no longer feel productive, a strong sense of meaninglessness occupies you and seems, in some cases, to result in an early death.

Is it possible for retirees to do without this need to produce? Some seem to manage by filling their agenda full of hustle. They plunge into indulgence as though their new product is to see it all and do it all before life nails the lid down. Their drive is narcotic. They need to enjoy more and more. Fun, fun, fun becomes their pursuit of happiness—too often a hapless pursuit. These perpetual-motion fun lovers cannot find enough fun in the world. Finally they are dissipated by cruises, tours, and sumptuous suppers. The gall bladder at last loads up with stones as an ordained signal that surfeiting is not happiness. And certainly in the quiet moments between such times there is the feeling that life should be lived in some more productive way. Lastly, the fear of utter loss usually begins to camp in the soul whose only product is self-indulgence. Those whose earlier quantum definition was that of a workaholic usually find it impossible to find a new fun-loving definition of themselves that they can live with. It is shallow and of no great appeal. I have observed that those who are productive till the end of life are less fearful of the end. Frequently, those who dread dying do so because they have lived without feeling they have ever really produced.

The leisure delusion falsely assumes that we are happiest when we have no need to be productive. Booker T. Washington's book *Up From Slavery* is the tale of a youth with a hunger to read and write.

On the day after the Emancipation Proclamation, young Booker is awakened by his mother, a slave, chasing down the rooster that had crowed and woke them. This same rooster crowed every morning and woke them before sunup to go into the fields. When Booker asks her why she is chasing the rooster, she says she is going to kill the rooster and cook it for dinner. "Mr. Lincoln done set us free," she cries to her son. "We don't have to go to them fields ever again if we don't want to!" But Booker's new leisure was but the place to address the meaning of his days. Time would be his now and he would not find leisure a rewarding place to live. Set free to choose how he would use his time, he decided to use it in disciplined ways.

There woke in Booker's life that morning a great longing to make his life usable to God and man. He desired to produce not just an education for himself but through Tuskegee Institute an education for all those who would come from the chains of slavery and learn a new way of life. The desire to produce flamed in his soul and he worked tirelessly, fueled by a great dream that matured under his ceaseless effort.[5]

There is no one so fortunate as the man whose dreams possess him. Dreams direct and manage. The cinema leap moves far ahead to beckon us on toward becoming all we can be. Dreams build into the dreamer a holy dissatisfaction with things as they are. Dreams propel us along the rails of destiny. A worthy dream acquires vigor and turns from the casual or easy. It is the dream that puts the passion into living. Most boredom that gives rise to the sweepstakes delusion comes from lives that pursue nothing with passion.

We all want to feel excitement about what we've chosen to do in life. Don Marquis wrote of a moth with whom he had a conversation. The moth was absurdly trying to "fry himself" on an electric light bulb. When asked why he felt such a compulsion to make a cinder of himself, the moth declared himself perfectly sane. He declared that he had plenty of common sense, but then he said, "At times we get tired of using it. We get bored with the routine and crave beauty and excitement. Fire is beautiful and we know that if we get too close it will kill us. But what does it matter? It is better to be happy for a moment and be burned up with beauty than to live a long time and be bored all the while."

Don Marquis could not bring himself to agree with the kamikaze moth. Still, he had to confess: "I wished there was something I wanted as badly as he wanted to fry himself."[6] The poet James Kavanaugh would certainly agree about the importance of passion to meaning in life. "I'm gonna sit here till passion returns ... I'm not going anywhere—even to death—Until I can go passionately."[7]

So many dead eyes in dead faces at closing times make it clear that too many are living without any passionate directing dream. Dreamless living is the parent of the sweepstakes delusion.

The leisure delusion and the drive for security both depend upon money. Security in financial areas depends on shrewd investment and tax sheltering. Of course financial security is meaningless without good health. But how much money does it take to be truly happy and enjoying all the leisure we would like? Just how much security is enough? One entrepreneur of our age replied to the question, "How much money does it take to be content? ... Just a little bit more!"

But those who have overprovided have to admit that, although they have amassed comfortable material goods, they tremble that they still may not have enough to last. So all their financial provisions are able to afford them only a neurotic joy. The impending terror of the golden years goes brass.

Leisure is a hurried demon! "Have fun," it cries, "but step on it! There isn't much time." Having fun in a hurry was reflected in a beer commercial some years ago, "You only go around once, so grab all the gusto you can!" The leisure seeker eyes the clock nervously and reminds himself that he must hurry if he is to manage to find time to indulge his every appetite. He must "Eat, drink, and be merry!" for tomorrow he must die. If he does not hurry he is likely to die without having all the pecan tortes he would have liked.

Living It Up and the End of Living

Such indulgent philosophies begin to show their weaknesses when death itself looms larger and nearer than the goodies of life. Despair over lost indulgence begins to set in. To see others win the sweepstakes while we have not even the necessary medicines to smile through our pain makes us want to cry like the writer of Ecclesiastes, "Emptiness of emptiness, all is emptiness!" (*see* 1:2). In the process of getting older we come to understand the foolishness of both the leisure delusion and the sweepstakes delusion. No inheritance is coming and what is coming may be terrifying. Our chances of cancer, a heart attack, and costly hospitalization are ever before us. None of us can escape it. George Bernard Shaw said, "Death is the ultimate statistic. It affects one out of one."

Our coming inheritance is not certain: death is! Carl Gustav Jung said that death is no paper tiger. Past the age of thirty-five, it is a common preoccupation of our minds. Our leisure is made neurotic by the constant inner threat of not being around anymore. This heavy reality rarely stops the person whose chief pursuit is leisure. It does not turn him to God; in fact it seems to drive him in a frenzy to hurry and enjoy. He does not think, "Since my final years are short, how can I use my final years to produce?" but rather, "How can I speed up the incoming comfort and enjoyment stimuli so as to 'grab all the gusto I can' "?

Nevil Shute's great novel, *On the Beach*, is a tale of life in Australia after the Northern Hemisphere has been obliterated in nuclear war. Bands of radiation, moved by prevailing winds, are slowly creeping southward toward Australia, the last continent containing uncontaminated human life. The Australians in this fictional account know that in a few brief months they will all be dead and human life will have perished from the earth. Their knowledge of the end neither turns them to God nor to a hurried sense of producing something real to leave behind. Rather, hedonism rages. The Australians in their final days turn to enjoyment.[8] This novelist obviously believes that neither death, nor its impending, changes values. Seeing the end only intensifies the values we already have.

During the Cuban missile crisis in the sixties, I was pastor of a congregation located only a few miles from the Strategic Air Command headquarters. Our whole nervous community waited out the president's embargo of Cuba. We were all asked to preserve extra drinking water and food. The uncertain warning caused a rush on the food stores.

One interesting facet of this epidemic was a rush to buy handguns and other kinds of firearms. It was obvious that many in our community were preparing to defend their homes and goods in extreme ways. The question was who were these food and gun hoarders going to shoot? Likely not the Russians. They would not be coming over on the missiles. All this firepower would be used against greedy neighbors and friends who might invade their larders after the holocaust.

Being unprepared to shoot Harry and Madge, our equally nervous next-door neighbors, I decided not to buy a gun. Nor did I buy an overlarge stash of food. I did call several local book and Bible stores to see if the crisis had precipitated any rush on Bibles. No bookstore reported that there had been one. Apparently most Americans were more interested in bullets than Bibles.

Grace and Greed

Why was I so insecure about Harry and Madge? They could, in a crisis, have anything we had. But I could not help wondering if, after the holocaust, I had gone to borrow a lead-shielded, isotope-free cup of milk, would Harry have fired on me? Would Madge have grenaded me? I could never quite see Harry and Madge the same way again. They were fine friends before the crisis, but while I could not remember if they had a Bible or not, I knew they had a gun.

Hoarding is always based on greed. It is a me-first preoccupation that says, "I must get my share of the goods before the 'greedy people' do."

Whence this fierce protectionism? Do we not all hold the view that goods are ultimate? Do crises change such views? No, there is within us the drive to defend to the end what is ours. Whether or not we actually shoot the neighbors in a crisis would probably be determined by the value we place on life as compared to the value we place on things.

The value that we place on things gets distorted in contemporary Christianity. This love of things inspires both work and the sweepstakes dream. It hurries our production to the point that we do not put our lives into our work. We work only to get and have . . . we hurry to work in order to have. As Paul Tournier says: "The yield of our life does not depend so much on the number of things that we do, but more on the quality of the self-giving we put into each thing. In order to add this quality, we must depart from the atmosphere of the modern world which is completely obsessed with activism, even in the church: do, do, do always more. Let us rather, once again, become inspired and tranquil men."[9]

But sudden inheritance does not make tranquil men. And the hope of inheritance produces only chills and fever. In this despair that claims our lives we turn to God's grace. Grace is preached nowadays as the bonanza that makes us not only more like Jesus but healthier and wealthier. God's saving grace has become in our culture a way "to keep from losing." It is, to use a Scott Peck phrase, a way to "cope with our impotence."

The world is complex and we can do little to change it or to make our own way in it. But scores of video evangelists remind us that if we but "accept Christ" all these other things will be added unto us (Matthew 6:33). We will no longer be impotent. Grace is the great sweepstakes and we hold the winning lottery ticket right in our baptismal certificate. Now God will dump on whatever material things we claim in prayer.

We once had a lecturer at our church who said that whenever he wanted a new suit that was out of his price range, he just walked about the rack on which it hung and claimed the suit as his own by the grace of God. This "name it and claim it" strategy had landed him quite a wardrobe, all of which, he said, had been spiritually furnished to him by a gracious God. His talk impressed me with the graciousness of God, but not necessarily the good taste of God, since most of his clothes seemed ill-tailored and poorly coordinated.

Still, his idea is strong among contemporary Christians. Many now believe that not only can we have whatever we ask for, but that all sickness and suffering can be avoided in the prayer of faith. Many believe that sickness clearly marks the disciple as one who has little faith, or God would have healed him. It is not the will of the Father that any should be sick.

Grace is the great bonanza! "Promises made in the name of faith range from the routine to the ridiculous, from 'God wants you well,' to, 'Everyone can own a Cadillac.' One evangelist recently announced that in his meeting God would fill teeth with gold and silver—the fillings being in the form of a cross."[10]

Such foolish notions overlook the significance of the cross itself. Grace itself is the gift. Christ is the gift. We do not accept Jesus because He is a doting Santa, but because He unites us with His Father, thus infusing all of life with spiritual meaning.

When Jesus Himself is the gift, then we do not ask to have life any wealthier or more painless than Jesus Himself had it. Poverty may be of some use to God in causing us to need Christ. Pain may be of use to God to build character within us. C. S. Lewis called suffering and hurt "the money on the game!"[11] Flannery O'Connor spoke of the "sweat and stink" of the cross.[12] Paul Billheimer reminds us: ". . . there is no character development without suffering. . . ."[13]

In the pain and hurt of life, our stick-out-ness is trimmed back. Our individuality becomes less important than our great need. Success needs are traded for simple survival. We thus become more real and our innate self grows reflective and God centered and our more brazen quantum self becomes meek and willing to listen for the footsteps of hope rather than pushing to succeed.

The opposite of the sweepstakes mentality in faith is outright crucifixion. On Good Friday Jesus does not win the bonanza. At the cross, Christ seems disinherited! He is naked. All that He owned is gone! There Christ models for us the transitoriness of all that can be owned. Only grace, then, matters! Bereft of this world's goods, He paves the way for us to understand what true inheritance is.

Three years prior to His death, Jesus was tempted in the desert. Jesus in the wilderness of temptation ends forever the sweepstakes delusion. As the Son of God at the moment of temptation, Jesus could have had anything. The point is not that He is tempted to make one stone into one loaf of bread. The inherent truth is that He can make every stone He wishes into bread. The issue for Jesus is the sweepstakes. All that He wants He can have. He has but to command it. If there was ever to be a time in His life when the material world could have been ultimate, surely this would be the time. But He came, not to teach self-indulgence, but self-denial. The character of a great person is not to be measured by what he gathers to himself, but by what he denies himself.

If there is any doubt that this intangible, spiritual substance is as real as money in the bank, one has only to look at the outstanding examples of Christians and martyrs throughout history. So often those whose lives are most clearly defined and powerfully influential are those whose total sacrifice of self left them utterly impoverished, but wealthy in influence beyond their most impressive dreams. How true the cliché: All you can hold in your cold, dead hand is what you have given away.

Spiritual product is more real than the material. Therefore spiritual product gives us a more genuine self-esteem. In the week we celebrated our twenty-fifth wedding anniversary, I met a nun who was celebrating her fiftieth year of "marriage to Christ." In her warm celebration of fifty years of ministry, I was confronted by her sacrifice, whose product made her seem wealthy and gave her a radiant contentment.

How different from this nun is the army of "Christian"

positivists who argue in glittering theology that to give is to get. Their doctrine is purely material. "God," they say, "sponsors no flops. He glories in making us rich. We are children of the King, and should on occasion flash a diamond or two to identify ourselves as royalty." Such video proponents of "success evangelism" often confuse the Via Dolorosa with Wall Street. They offer a self-esteem based on tycoon management and entrepreneurial prayer.

"God will make your business prosper," they say, or, "For every dollar you send me, God will repay you tenfold." These "spiritual sweepstakers," by their own logic, would only have to mail each of their supporters a dollar to step blissfully to opulence. Rich corporations have taught financial pyramiding as the way "to taste and see that the Lord is good." Many who succumb to the golden gospel do so with the same hope that a sweepstakes hopeful purchases a lottery ticket.

Conclusion

Will instant inheritance provide you with self-esteem? Wealth is product, but instant, inherited substance will not produce any lasting feelings of self-esteem. The innate self will judge it at last as shallow and the quantum self will find product without struggle adds nothing to be measured. The sweepstakes is all too automatic and requires too little discipline from which lasting feelings of self-esteem can derive.

But hard work and product are fully complemented by the self-esteem you can find in God's grace. Grace esteem builds in you a feeling of great worth precisely because you cannot earn it. You are loved and called a son by God Himself. Loved by the greatest of lovers, you can love yourself. There is a strong relationship between grace and product. You will want to produce great things in your life—not so God will love you but because He does. The glory of the sweepstakes can be forgotten, for the treasure of His grace is reason enough to think well of yourself. With such strong reasons to believe in yourself, you can outgrow your need for the spurious meaning of the sweepstakes delusion.

7

Integrate
or
Disintegrate

This I most humbly require and desire of you all, even for his sake who is the God of us all, that I be not compelled to the thing which my conscience doth repugn or strive against.

John Huss

Little turtle,
who has turned you upside down?
Did you come into the open once too often?
Did life find you out?

Donna Swanson, *Mind Song*

This above all: to thine own self be true
And it must follow, as the night the day,
Thou canst not then be false to any man.

William Shakespeare, *Hamlet*

Integration is the process of bringing opposite values together and making them one. The self you cherish will disintegrate unless you can integrate two important areas. First you must integrate your drive to succeed with the issue of not taking your success too seriously. Second you must integrate praise and personal criticism in such a way as to improve without destroying yourself. Let us turn first to the issue of your own success and the need to lessen the heavy demands you place upon yourself.

Unexpected cardiac arrest is the most common cause of death in America and Monday is the day it most generally occurs. "Every week, over eight thousand Americans die suddenly of heart attacks. This in itself is a sobering statistic. But it becomes even more alarming when we consider that far more of these deaths occur on Monday than on any other day (*American Medical News,* May 15, 1981). Why Monday? Because it is the first workday of the week—the day when American workers abandon the relaxing pace of a weekend at home and return to the pressures of life on the job."[1] Work itself is a stimulus to meaning. It is therefore a strong stimulus to life. But work becomes a killer when it leads us to compete with deadlines and the stern demands of the clock. Clocks measure our work in segments. With only two hands and twelve numbers they rivet our eyes to their leering dials, reminding us that we have either succeeded or failed their narrow deadlines. Their black fingers point out our shame or our glory. Popular singer Dolly Parton wrote the song "9 to 5," the anthem of secretarial stress in corporations. And the stress, as the movie humorously pointed out, is not always humorous.

Lewis Mumford went so far as to say: "The clock, not the steam engine, is the key machine of the industrial age."[2] And G. A. Woodcock pointed to the destructive, disintegrating power of the clock when he wrote: "The clock represents an element of mechanical tyranny in the lives of modern man more potent than any individual exploiter or any other machine."[3] But why should deadlines have such power over us? What is it that clocks do? Clocks measure segments of our lives that we wish to use in the building of our various life-styles and dreams. The more we invest in our dreams, the more urgently we obey the clock. So in reality it is the clock plus our personal ambition that builds stress into our lives.

Most of us disintegrate by inches. We erode emotionally and physically because of our insane concern about deadlines. If you are prone to doubt this, think of those few times in life when you've been forced to live without your wristwatch for a single day. The likelihood is that you frequently "called time" or asked your secretary what time it was. This no-watch neurosis is born in our need to be "on time." Like the March Hare, we click along freeways wailing, "I'm late, I'm late."

Unselfing: Integrating Criticism and Praise

How can you beat the clockwork bind? Since you cannot rid the world of clocks and watches, maybe you could do what Eugene Peterson suggests: "America is in conspicuous need of unselfing. Concerned observers using the diagnostic disciplines of psychology, sociology, economics and theology lay the blame for the deterioration of our public life and the disintegration of our personal lives at the door of the self...."[4] The clocks would be of less concern to you if you could "unself" and free yourself of an overserious agenda.

To manage this "unselfing" you would have to quit pushing yourself and those around you with demands and deadlines. Those few who do handle life's heavy demands frequently head organizations where they place intolerably heavy demands upon underlings. Fred Friendly of CBS was once asked if he had ever had a nervous breakdown. "No, but I'm a carrier," he replied.[5]

Unselfing will always require an integration of personal agenda and the wider, fuller meaning of life. When life in its greatness is stirred into your furious little dreams, this integration will occur. But if you keep only a narrow focus, you had best watch out for Monday mornings or be sure you golf with a cardiologist.

In short, you must integrate or disintegrate. You must learn this integration as early as possible in life. Unfortunately, high-agenda parents are usually "carriers" of nervous conditions that they pass on to their children at early ages. Some years ago, a six-year-old girl in the congregation I serve was sent by her parents to a psychiatrist for treatment. What prompted her referral? All the factors would be difficult to chart. In her quiet nature she had become so withdrawn she seemed no longer present in the world. Her parents' drive to make her a model child caused them to coerce her behavior rather than correct it. Her self-esteem was destroyed. She developed a sense of futility to the point that she felt she could do nothing to win their pleasure or acceptance. But psychotherapy did its work. Once unacceptable to her parents, she became acceptable to herself.

These parents themselves were selfish because they had never known much love. Earl Wilson has written: "I have discovered an interesting thing about selfish people. They do not feel loved. In fact, the more selfish they are, the less loved they feel; and the less loved they feel, the more selfish they become. It is a vicious circle."[6] In this case, the vicious circle was devouring every possible hope of the child's self-esteem.

I once counseled a small and fragile woman whose irate, bearlike husband abused her. She was too frightened of his reprisals to ask for help (mine or anyone else's). In a moment of desperate daring, at last she summoned the courage to ask me for help. Her husband found out and was predictably angry. Fortunately he took it out on me rather than her. He struck me on the jaw, knocking me to the floor. By the time I came to, his anger had cooled and he apologized and agreed to counseling. His was a clear case of poor self-image that had caused him to intimidate his wife's compliant nature to the detriment of them both.

These cases clearly indicate what happens to the human spirit which is forced to produce without any sense of integration or affirmation. Hard drivers are usually hard to discourage. The person who never hears negative feedback becomes, in time, the grand intimidator of others. The grand intimidator drives without any corrective input. Neither the intimida*tor* nor the intimida*tee* really produce much worthwhile in life. The intimida*tee* is so steeped in inferiority that he rarely sees anything worthy in his life. The arrogant driver, on the other hand, overrates the value of his product. His worldview is so superficial he cannot be goaded into believing he might actually do something to improve what he produces.

Criticism is the all-powerful weapon of the hard driver. Criticism can function in terms of our self-improvement. Personal growth and progress is always better learned from those who criticize you than those who affirm you. Even a venomous and destructive attack upon you or on any of the product of your life may hold within its venom the seeds of some renewing truth. But you must consider the reason and the source of criticism when it comes your way. You must have the courage to stand against any purely demeaning attack. You need to remember that the superachiever who sees other people as fuel for his success machine offers criticism as a way of managing you and not helping you understand who you are.

Let us here consider the second aspect of your integration: balancing praise and criticism. *How you integrate affirmation and criticism determines if you win or lose in life.* Integrating these negative and positive words is an evidence of mental health. You must deal with truth as people who are true. If you build too heavily on negative feedback, you will arrive at a deficient self-concept! Worse, you will be accepting a lie as the basis of your self-view.

Is such a statement fair? Are those who give you only negative feedback concerning yourself or your product really lying to you? Yes, not necessarily because all or any part of their criticism is a lie, but by giving you only one kind of feedback, they soon cause you to see yourself in ways that are false.

The "I'm OK—You're OK" philosophy which we will be

discussing later in this chapter is rooted in the simplicity of this imperative balance. It is Aunt Eller who sings in *Oklahoma* these fantastic words of balance:

> *I'd like to teach you all a little sayin'*
> *And learn the words real proper like you should;*
> *I may not be no better than anybody else,*
> *But I'll be durned if I'm not just as good.*[7]

Or who can forget this little jingle?

> *There's so much good in the worst of us*
> *and so much bad in the best of us*
> *That it hardly behooves the most of us*
> *To talk about the rest of us.*

I was once entertained for dinner at the warden's residence while I was visiting a New England prison. The butler so filled me with awe at his social gifts that I was stunned when the warden told me that this gentle man was once a savage ripper. Suddenly the simple knife with which he carved the dinner roast seemed sinister.

Savagery and service may abide within the same soul. Man has a propensity for good or evil. It is small wonder that Luther referred to man as *simul justus et peccator* (at once saint and sinner), for in truth we are capable of glory or horror. The effect of too much affirmation and too much criticism is the same. The person in either case is rendered useless. It is the issue of product: The overaffirmed person loses his sense of evaluation and cannot really tell if his product is good or not. The overcriticized cannot see any good at all in his product and hence cannot believe in himself. It is imperative, therefore, that you learn to integrate feedback.

Overaffirming, Underaffirming

Let me offer two concrete examples at either end of the spectrum. First, let us look at the overaffirmed.

Her name was Jennie. She was adopted and long awaited by parents in their mid-thirties. While she had three adopted older brothers, she was the first girl to come into the home. Never was a baby more welcome. I watched their joy at their new daughter and participated with them in that joy. But early in the little girl's development I became wary. Her parents belonged to the "Rolls-Royce social set." They denied her nothing, complimented her profusely, and celebrated her continuously with their friends. Most of their friends were mid-lifers like themselves and had earlier raised their own children to the teen years. Suddenly the emergence of Jennie as an ill-disciplined teenager caused most of their friends to withdraw in horror.

By early adolescence, the girl was dating whomever she wished with little advice and no parental admonishment. In fact, her dates were celebrated, financed, and enjoyed. Curfews were broken; late night vigils set in and gradually it became apparent that "the proper girl" raised in an upper-income home had become unmanageable.

Finally, the parents began to tighten up. They adopted this new policy to save her from an increasingly promiscuous life-style. The new clamps only served to separate her more fully from her parents. And at last, in a moment of anger, she confessed to them she was pregnant. They wept. She dashed it all off as their fault. She then ran off with an illegal alien and lived with him outside the country till the baby was born. The parents rarely saw her after that.

It is difficult in such a life to see any product at all. Jennie was a most talented girl and brought tears to the eyes of those who heard her singing in the church. But she was too much praised. She learned none of the lessons that a critical look at her talent might have taught. Her usefulness to God or society was and is to this moment lost.

She received only positive feedback. The quantum self inflated, a typical fault among teenagers whose inner innate self is not mature enough to hold a billowing pride in check. What easily develops among overaffirmed teenagers might be termed by the less refined as the "snot nose" syndrome—a flippant self-image where the outer quantum self struts in naive glory.

Just as Jennie was an example of the overaffirmed, Graham will illustrate the underaffirmed. Graham was a last-minute menopause baby. Throughout his childhood, his father called him "the surprise"—unwanted, unwelcome! Like Jennie's parents, Graham's were also fairly well-off. Although they lived in Harlem, his father owned a fleet of trucks that provided the family with a far better living than most of the other blacks living around them. Graham therefore was indulged by his father, who often felt guilty over the way he treated Graham and atoned for his abusiveness by surfeiting his son with the good things of life, such as a brand-new car during his high school years. His mother also felt guilty for not protecting Graham against his father's sullen outrages, and indulged the boy herself.

Before any group, the boy would weep and break into tears if asked to make a speech or give a book report. But individually, Graham could make quite an impression. He had the wheels and cash to drive the fast lane, break curfews, and soak himself in the drug culture. All of these offenses drove his parents to a rage. He came to actual fistfights with his father, and their abrasive confrontations at last resulted in a kind of truce—Graham joined the army and was sent, after basics, to Vietnam. His belligerence made him into an aggressive fighter. Before he finally came home, he was wounded three times, and decorated for his courage.

Gradually, however, he became a recluse after his military service. Tired of fighting, his search for fulfillment and meaning in life went unfulfilled. Often depression colored his mood with such severity he was immobilized. He worked at menial jobs (though his IQ was high). Victimized by low self-esteem, he met and slept with various live-in girl friends. Their tenderness toward him supplied more touch and understanding than he had ever known at home. His loose morality offended his church-attending parents, but his many sexual consorts offered him a kind of self-esteem. Ultimately he converted to Christianity and began to feel that his love of Christ demanded that he prepare himself to become a pastor.

He was accepted at an Ivy League divinity school, but even as a seminarian, he found it impossible to forgive his abusive father.

It happened in time that his father became ill with a carcinoma that forced Graham, out of conscience, to pay him a visit in the hospital. Ravaged by disease, his father was no longer an intimidating physical giant. As Graham approached him, the father began weeping. Graham was touched to hear his father begging his forgiveness. The reconciliation of this ill-used son with his prodigal father set the young man free. Through his new relationship with Christ and his father's penitent attitude, Graham began to change into a more assertive man.

It did not immediately increase the amount of product in his life, but his parents' new esteem for him eventually matured Graham into a scholar, thinker, and counselor. Graham's transformation produced a love for all he met as well as a ready interest in the lives and problems of others. The existence of his natural understanding of the love he felt for others had long been smothered by his own inner anger and what the Bible calls a "root of bitterness" (Hebrews 12:15) toward his father.

This bitter root that once sent tentacles of venom throughout the soil of all his relationships is now gone. The pain and insecurity of his early years has toughened and matured his innate self. Graham now heads a prestigious counseling practice in Manhattan and his counselees are his product. The gentle but wise character of his counsel is an effective product that makes his quantum self both commanding and affectionate. He is admired and thus admires himself. He has been able to integrate his years of negative conditioning with a positive future. He cannot change his past or repair all that had happened, but he can mix them together in such a way as to find out who he is.

Integrating: Surviving Negative Feedback

This has been one of the strong tenets of Thomas A. Harris in his book *I'm OK, You're OK.* Harris says there are only four possible life positions.[8] One can say, "I'm OK, you're not OK," which is a judgment of superiority (and as we already said, is a liar's way). Or we can say, "I'm not OK, you're OK," which is a definition of low self-esteem. Again such a view comes from an inadequate sense of product and too little self-esteem. One can also say, "I'm not OK, you're not OK," which is a sociopathic condition.

But the final and healthiest kind of statement comes from the person who says, "I'm OK, you're OK." This kind of statement comes from a person who has integrated his good and bad character traits and still accepts himself. Such integration is the frontispiece to sound self-esteem and is based on an acceptance for the appreciation of one's life and all it produces.

Most communication that you receive comes in terms of two readings: friendly communication (communiqués that affirm) and unfriendly communication (communiqués that undermine your self-esteem). These messages can be oral-audible or body-language messages. In terms of self-esteem, these messages are critical in the early years of formation.

But the real issue of whether you are able to arrive at self-esteem lies more in the way you integrate feedback than in the nature of the communiqué. As a pastor, I long ago discovered that I could help others integrate feedback through positive analysis. I had a very young friend in the church whose name was Barry. Barry was an incredible athlete and his father took pleasure only in this one aspect of his life. Barry was too slight to become a major power in the world of college or pro football, but throughout junior high and high school he played tennis extremely well. He won the state tennis finals his junior year. So he got plenty of needed affirmation from those matches.

Tennis was Barry's way to shine, and the applause of the crowd said to Barry, loud and clear, "Your product is good." Still, his father rarely said, "Barry, you did a good job," or "You played well." He was far more prone to say, "Why do you hug the net when your opponent is at the baseline, you idiot?" Barry knew he had to answer the question because his father communicated with an abusive style. If he did not answer, his father would slap him or slam him up against the wall and curse his silence. If he did say, "I don't know, Dad. It seemed right at the time," his father would bellow, "Right at the time—you fool! How could it seem right, you idiot? Answer me that!" More cursing followed.

Barry's father came across as one long, ugly communiqué of power. He was a big man with a gruff voice, forty pounds overweight, yet somehow not flabby. He had an office in one room of his house, which was off limits to any of his nine children or timid wife. He had a splendid gun collection. The blue-steel barrels of his guns rose like cathedral organ pipes behind his desk, and he was forever cleaning them. The vision I remember of this hulk of a man sitting behind his huge desk cleaning a big gun sends a chill through me even yet. His family lived daily under this chilling image.

Barry was a miracle to me. He lived for his mother, who was kept busy with housekeeping and family and could expect no help from the big man in his gun-walled office. Whenever she fed her brood, she had to be sure she had all meals ready on time for her "fee-fie-fo" husband. She was so intimidated by life that she endured this misery, refusing to try to make her way with the children on her own. But she was as good to the children as she could be in that kind of house.

A Sunday-school bus stopped and picked up Barry's family every Sunday morning. A few weeks after meeting them, I became friends with Barry. He was hungry for friendship with an affirming man, and eagerly took me up on my offer to buy him a Coke after tennis practice. I could not know that these Cokes made him an hour late getting home, and he had to face King Kong, whose interrogations revealed Barry had been spending time with a Baptist preacher. "Why in hell would any grown man wanna spend time with you? Better watch a man who likes boys!" he shouted at Barry.

Finally, Barry had enough! At the risk of never seeing his mother and siblings again, he left home. He continued in school, living with whoever could make a place for him. His father had always told him, "The door swings only one way here! Leave any time you want to, but you'll never get back in!" He was a man of his ugly word, and Barry knew it. The only good thing about his father was that he never—true to his word—tried to chase Barry down after he left home. He was relieved to no longer be responsible for the boy. Barry, in spite of his homelessness, seemed to have a glint of happiness. "I miss Mom and the kids," he said, "but I guess it's better this way." A Japanese family who lived only a few blocks from their home allowed him sleeping space and he got a job at a service station and finished high school. His marks were so good that he won a scholarship to M.I.T., where he did well academically and made the tennis team in his sophomore year.

The incredible thing was that he managed to make it. He was most popular at high school and warmly received at church. But most impressive to me is that he remains, to this date, the best example of integration and adjustment I have ever seen. In his life there was great product but little affirmation. He was able to blend this small affirmation into a whole view of himself and thus find meaning and purpose in life.

Julia was another matter, unable to survive early negative abuse. She had been a ward of the Illinois state courts at four, along with an older brother. Her foster parents had first seen her on the front page of a Chicago newspaper—she was barely recognizable as a little girl because of cigarette burns all over her body. Her face had few burns (as is almost always the case), but showed some bruises and signs of cartilage and structural damage. Her brother clearly was battered as well.

Jim Thomas, her soon-to-be foster father, was touched by the plight of these children and did his utmost to win the right to become the new parents of these battered children. Jim and his wife had not been able to have children of their own, and these children became for them a way to have an immediate family. The Thomases were all this pair of battered children could hope for. They readily confessed that they found it hard to speak roughly to these timid siblings. The scars on their thin bodies were such a powerful reminder of the children's ill-fortune they could not often bring themselves to correct them.

Their love did have a strong influence on these children who, upon first entering their new home, were shy and afraid of the Thomases and all other adults. Gradually, the children seemed to adjust and learned to achieve. Julia began piano lessons and became very good at music. She preferred somber music; still, in her teen years she seemed to progress toward a healthy self-image. But as she grew older she became once more reclusive.

The Thomases bore a heavy burden during her final years at home. Away at college, beyond the reach of their support and constant affirmation, she became increasingly withdrawn. Finally, signs of moroseness faded into psychotic depressive behavior and then a total break with reality. She has for the past several years been in and out of hospitals, unable to make her own way in the world. (Her older brother has had some of the same psychotic symptoms, although not to the degree of Julia's.)

Julia was given, during her years with the Thomases, continual affirmation, but her early years with her real parents prevented her from integrating the positive stimuli of her adoptive parents in sufficient strength to survive. She literally disintegrated over a series of years and the disintegration was impossible to stop.

Why did Barry survive while Julia did not? Barry succeeded by using four principles that you must incorporate into your own life.

First, Barry was able to celebrate his innate self even when his quantum self was under siege. He knew because of his faith that he was worth something to God, and this inner celebration was attached firmly to the innate self at such moments as when his tennis prowess was being put down.

Second, Barry was able to see that his stick-out-ness (athletic ability) was affirmed by his tennis fans. He could celebrate his athletic prowess on the inside even when he dared not mention this inner celebration to his critical father.

Third, he recognized that his father was impossible to please. No matter what Barry or anyone else might do, it would not elicit approval from a man who communicated only negativity or outright abuse. Much as Barry might want the approval of his own father, he was able to see how much his father's reaction differed from that of all the other people around him.

Finally, Barry could extend the compliments far enough to stand up for himself. "I'm OK" was the self-evaluation he accepted when he had integrated all the incoming data.

These four principles are: 1. understanding your own inner worth; 2. making sure the evidence of criticism does not overshadow the frequency of affirmation; 3. a consideration of the source of both criticism and praise; 4. a thoughtful integration of all incoming data.

The cases we have just examined are, of course, extreme for the sake of establishing definitions. In most cases, such abusive kinds of feedback are missing. The positive communiqués we receive are more easily and quickly absorbed. Still, the facts remain, the better a person is at evaluating his own product and integrating the positive and negative feedback along with it, the better are his chances of survival and adjustment.

Marriage: The Nourisher of Self-Esteem

Marriage can be a matrix of glory in this regard. I confess that as a writer, I have always quailed before the process of mailing in manuscripts and waiting for evaluation. Like most writers, I had, at the beginning of my writing career, a significant amount of failure. Most of my feedback established in my mind the definite sensation that I could never master the art. Set against many rejection slips was my wife's opinion: Your writing is great! She was faithful in the typing of each new work, as confident and bright with hope at each new submission as I was. But it was not her joy at typing each new piece that sustained me, but her support when the piece came back with the "I'm sorry" clipped to the top.

She would often look at the memo and say, "Someday they'll be sorry—they'll beg you to write something for their lousy magazine—don't you do it—do you hear?—not one word!" I always promised her that when the day came that they begged me, I would turn my back on them and walk briskly away. I confess that her image of my heartless, ruthless turning away fed my spirits!

It never happened quite as she promised. I still have not enjoyed the grasping feel of an editor groveling on the ground before me, begging me for a paragraph to enlighten his life or magazine. But they have now written me and asked me to do articles, and I am always overjoyed when they do. I have now integrated all these rejection slips into the mix of my wife's great "strokes" until I have both a strong view of my talent and the weaknesses it must yet overcome.

The way that marriage really serves in this adjustment-integration and product mix can be demonstrated by the Curies or the Leakeys or any number of historical couples who, affirming and blessing each other's work, brought their world to new levels of excellence. I was struck by the powerful historical evaluations of Will and Ariel Durant. In one of their last books was the statement, "I pray that if I die first the whole of this work will come to fruition at last in you." The power of this simple blessing is proof enough that happily married couples find immense product and affirmation in their relationship and thus move on to strong self-esteem.

One of my favorite examples of this is in the life of Robert and Elizabeth Barrett Browning. Elizabeth Barrett was not abused as a child, but she did live in the home of a tyrannical father. Her brothers adjusted better than she did, for their lives soon held promise of leaving home and his pernicious influence. Elizabeth had no such hope. Her invalid view of herself perhaps contributed to her becoming an invalid. Her quiet and beautiful acquiescence brooded poetically. Her innate self soared. In the excellence of her product, perhaps, her own quiet self-acceptance was born. Yet it was bathed in doubt—self-doubt that made her reluctant to show her poetry to Robert once they had become acquainted.

Her self-doubt was swallowed up in his magnificent affirmation. His love for her and her work caused her own self-esteem to rise. After their elopement to Italy, she became brighter in spirit. She began to develop her quantum self as she accepted Robert's admiration for her life product. Her verses, like her legs, grew stronger and for the last ten years of her life she walked normally.

For every tale like this there are, of course, the opposite ones of marital abuse and low self-esteem. Still, a good marriage is possible. But it is rare that a marital partner is sensitive enough and affirming enough to supply all the strokes self-esteem requires. Too often husbands and wives compete so fiercely with each other that neither offers many compliments.

Married or not, every ego itself becomes responsible for its own grand adjustment. The number one issue is, "What is so special about me?" And the number two issue is, "What is so special about my product?" The answer to this question becomes more meaningful as the producer compares his product with what he sees around him.

Artistic Self-Esteem

When the child with an artistic bent brings home his first stick-figure drawing, he feels good about it because his teacher said it was good. But he also feels good about it because he sits by James and (in his overegoed judgment) his picture seems so much better than James's. As he continues to draw and paint, his frame of reference expands. At fourteen he compares himself with the best of the fourteen-year-old artists he knows and it seems to him, as a high school sophomore, he is keeping pace.

In college and later art shows, he continually compares himself with artists and rates himself up or down, depending on his subject matter, media, and technique. If he continues to drive himself, he soon cares less for his critics' remarks than the quality he sees in those standards he has developed.

The wider his understanding of the field, the more he is able to compare and place himself in the field.

If he is rated down, he excuses himself by a (sometimes right) judgment that his critics lack understanding and cannot judge properly since their frame of reference is not as broad as his. If he is put down in a press review, he will likely (and maybe rightly) say,"What do they know?" Such an attitude can degenerate to cynicism.

The best artists (nearly all who make their mark) have to deal with this. Cynicism can accompany those who receive too much rejection. But the best manage a level of adjustment that says, "If I want my product respected is it not fair to show respect for others' art?" Peter Shaffer's fine play *Amadeus* reminds us that such is not absolutely necessary, for Mozart often held others in contempt while believing himself to be the only true genius he knew.[9] Frank Lloyd Wright once referred to himself in public as the world's greatest living architect, to which his wife remonstrated, "Frank, you shouldn't have said that!" "What?" he demurred. "Did you expect me to perjure myself in front of all those people?"

Most of the time, if the product is impressive, we are reluctant to criticize the producer even if he is arrogant. We still operate out of the old adage—"If you done it, you ain't braggin'!" Lee Iacocca's autobiography is sometimes marked by arrogance, yet it seems forgivable in the wake of his marvelous achievements.

Most of the time the respect we have for others is responsible for the path we take to our own destiny. We are following a technique called "copy and innovate" to self-respect. There is, as has been said, little that is truly original. Product comes from our lives by comparing and imitating with some innovation. One is reminded that Shakespeare did not create Romeo and Juliet. He borrowed the story from an Italian source and innovated. Leonard Bernstein in *West Side Story* did not wholly produce the Sharks and Jets from the Capulets and Montagues of Shakespeare. Each copied, yet each modified. It surely goes without saying that the original Italian source was not wholly original, but was itself likely an innovative copy of something prior.

At any rate, all artists in their time find self-esteem in their innovation and not in the copy. Each integrates his criticisms, mixes them with the affirmation of his product, and, presto, the history of literature and beautiful ideas continues to move forward.

Conclusion

There is a power in you that allows you to integrate your abuses and compliments and arrive at a concept of your product that makes you believe, "I am alive and the world is better for it!"

The issue of whether the world will be better because you live never derives from yourself. It comes largely from the integration of positive and negative feedback. You may know the exact place where the blessings or cursings will come. You learn early the best ways to avoid criticism and enjoy and prolong the compliment.

Dealing with criticism and affirmation is like eating a piece of cake. You may choose to eat the frosting only or the cake only. But cake, like life, is designed to be entirely consumed. The person who has never learned to eat some cake along with the frosting is a person who does not deal realistically with the various setbacks of life. Lee Iacocca reminds us in his autobiography, "Setbacks are a natural part of life, and you've got to be careful how you respond to them."[10] If you can integrate and keep on producing at the same time, you have learned the secret of the integrated life. Again it is Iacocca who reminds us that if you are integrated, "You learn to scramble and move quickly. You learn to produce. . . ."[11] This sense of product convinces those around you that you are a winner—they become convinced, but not on the basis of your integration, for they may not know this intrinsically. They become convinced on the basis of your product—is it good?—is it always coming off the line? Is it interrupted or terminated by the knocks and setbacks?

It was one of the European composers who reminded his son, whose new composition had received a very critical review, "Son, nobody ever built a statue of a critic." It was Theodore Roosevelt who said:

> It is not the critic who counts; not the man who points out how the strong man stumbled or where the doer of deeds could have done them better. The credit belongs to the man who is actually in the arena; whose face is marred by dust and sweat and blood; who strives valiantly; who errs, and comes up short again and again, because there is no effort without error and shortcoming; who does actually try to do the deed; who knows the great enthusiasm, the great devotion and spends himself in a worthy cause; who, at the worst, if he fails, at least fails while daring greatly.
>
> Far better it is to dare mighty things, to win glorious triumphs even though checkered by failure, than to rank with those poor spirits who neither enjoy nor suffer much because they live in the gray twilight that knows neither victory or defeat.[12]

He is very probably right. The gray-area lives have not been able to integrate the bumps and blessings and hence have not been able to make anything of life or of themselves. Not having created product, they have been unable to see their own place in the world. They could not fit it all together.

First it was they themselves who turned gray. They left the arena of real living and producing. Nothing of value was accomplished after they lost the color in their own lives.

It is even as Lord Fauntleroy said, "The world should be a little better because a man has lived."[13] Perhaps the world is better when we can see what we make. As you become a maker, you strengthen your sense of self. You can happily put Lord Fauntleroy's statement in a better tense: "The world *will* be a little better because I have lived."

8

Putting Narcissus in His Place

We live, deaf to the land beneath us,
Ten steps away no one hears our speeches.

Olga Ivinskaya, *A Captive of Time*

Men are but children of a larger growth.

Dryden, *All for Love*

But we also knew that Henry's decisions were not open to debate. As he liked to remind us, his name was on the building.

Lee Iacocca, *Iacocca: An Autobiography*

Narcissus is that egotistic youth in Greek mythology who so loved himself he drowned in the attempt to embrace his own reflection in a pool. Narcissus always wastes love in a foolish infatuation with himself. His egotism corrupts his affection. His vision is distorted. His romance is perverted! He is all that matters—he is the most handsome and intelligent of souls—just ask him!

His whole self-love affair is a sordid lie—an erotic lie that is totally inside himself. The inner lie is the worst lie, for it loses sight of all truth about the self and then becomes false to its world. One of the epigrams of chapter seven speaks Shakespeare's solid warning to Narcissus: "This above all: to thine own self be true. . . . Thou canst not then be false to any man."[1]

The inner lie excuses its falsity so that it sometimes becomes indistinguishable from the truth. But Narcissus rarely examines the issue of his inner integrity. He plays too much with his errant outer image to go very deep in life. Fascinated with his surface image, he sees himself as the center of the universe. He can manage a thin film of concern for others that gives him a relational context in his world. But he sees his world only as the soil that holds the roots of his all-important self.

You must understand that you—like everyone else—are a candidate for narcissism. You are well on the way toward narcissism when you begin to see persons as caste. When you most admire those in the upper strata of society, your quantum self can be in danger of spoiling itself. If those further down the social scale are less important to you because they can do less for you, you may have begun the drift. If your castelike overview becomes immoral, you will see people no longer for their own sake but only for what use you may make of them.

You must try to remember that Narcissus's glorious opposite is the person whose servanthood tries to lift others, not to make some use of them, but to help them find the best life they can. Narcissus cannot imagine knowing people for such a selfless reason.

Beware attachment to yourself! Your own self-fascination can quickly become hypnotic! From thinking well of yourself it is but a short path to thinking too well of yourself. Your life then can become a monologue—no other petty actors will matter in your show. Such arrogance is a "Liar's Show." Some psychologists suggest that all arrogance is lying. It is the great cover-up for the frightened psyche hiding inside of us. Narcissus feels more comfortable faking superiority than he does letting others see his intimidated self. At the quaking core of most arrogant personalities is a terrified person!

The Fuels of Arrogance

There are two fuels for arrogance. First of all, Narcissus is usually created by a life without trial. This easy-come world has brought him a full indulgence in the seldom-denied appetites of living. He has infrequently known the pain of rejection or having to do without. It isn't so much that he doesn't realize the existence of such pain, it's just that it has come to him only in minimal doses. Most of those who care about the fallen have known the pain of falling.

The other fuel of arrogance is the opposite of a life without pain. This Narcissus is acting out a vengeful dream of overcoming a great and abrasive pain he received as a child. Adolf Hitler's abusive tyranny may have derived from seeing his father assault and rape his mother. Some psychoanalysts believe that the abuses of Hitler's father turned Adolf into a frenzied achiever who longed all his life to get even.[2] Sigmund Freud may not have been a Narcissus in the same way that Adolf Hitler was, but his driving passion to achieve in life was marked by his father's dire prediction: "The boy will amount to nothing."[3] Woodrow Wilson's driving ambition to succeed may also have been an attempt to "get even" with his overdominant father, who severely damaged his self-esteem as a child.[4]

Narcissus, however, is blindly different from the self-effacing model of Woodrow Wilson. Narcissus is a zealot—ambitious for himself alone. But is Narcissus a producer? The arrogant person does not become so because of his exceptional product. His hyper-pride comes only because he overcelebrates what he does make. The person with low self-esteem may actually produce more than Narcissus. He, by contrast, undercelebrates. Both the proud and the whipped sin against self-image.

Narcissism! What is it classically? It is an autoerotic perversion. It is not hetero, not homo, only *auto*sexual. Narcissus gazes upon his own reflection, desires, and drowns. Is *auto*sexuality a real category? It is. It is the lust and passion of the inner lie. Autosexuality is as erotic in its own way as the more sensuous categories of love. But self-lust has no physiology—elated pride is the only gratification of its passion.

William James once wrote that all of us have any number of social selves. Perhaps the worst thing to be said of the ardent Narcissus is that he has lost his social soul. Really, he has lost all society. He seeks no social place he does not control or at least mine for his own treasure. When the recognition of others comes too slowly, his ravenous ego will compliment itself. When all outer affirmation quits, he doesn't mind altogether for it provides him a chance to be alone with his favorite person.

Narcissism is, after all, the "Me" generation. The Me generation has hosts of moderns sitting in designer jeans gazing at their rock-star alter egos. They throng Wall Street. They are the yuppies (young urban professionals)! The entrepreneurs! The queens of the business and professional world!

Alexander wept at thirty-three because there were "no more worlds to conquer." I recently sat with a twenty-four-year-old millionaire who was troubled because he seemed to be running out of ladder rungs on his *Wall Street Journal* climb to power. His meteoric rise to the state of "no more worlds to conquer" had eclipsed Alexander by nine years. We did not sit long, however. This Narcissus was a type-A workaholic on his way to some envisioned throne: He had little time for "trivial conversation." As his pastor, I was counseling him to mix a little of God into his recipe for success.

But at the very mention of his need for God, he roared away in his Lincoln Continental.

Angling

Proud yuppie millionaires always raise the question: Is it possible to love your self without arrogance? It is normal to want to be celebrated. But if you are not careful, you may soon begin fishing for compliments at the deep piers of ego.

You know the gear you need for that kind of fishing. You refer to a particular softball game where you hit three home runs. You never refer to the home runs; you supply the conversational bait to which a well-meaning friend can only reply, "Wasn't that the game where you hit three home runs?" Then you may modestly duck your head, shuffle your feet, and say, "Actually, I had forgotten about that."

Compliment fishing is done in two modes. There is what I like to think of as "dangling angling," where the bait is dangled into a large pool of peers after sufficient coaching is laid down. Amanda Winfield in *The Glass Menagerie* had rehearsed her Southern Belle mystique with her crippled daughter for years. In the gallery of her own mind she retained the image of herself as a young girl on a plantation porch surrounded by "gentlemen callers." The greatest Sunday afternoon she ever had as a young girl was the day she had "seventeen gentlemen callers" at one time. She is much older at the time of the setting of the play, but she has engineered her children and friends—and she has few—to snap at the bait of her long-ago, youthful triumph. She has but to mention any part of her youth, and her children and friends remind her of her greatest conquest—"Wasn't that the day that your seventeen gentlemen callers came?"[5]

"Dangling angling" is a game "played by tape" as Eric Berne, the psychologist, would say. It is played with predictable communication responses, and you can be sure that the responses are extremely predictable.

The dangling bait	*The angling snag*
"Madge, can you find Consolidated's file?"	"Sure, Boss . . . wasn't that the company that gave you the plaque last year?"
"Momma, where's my blue and white skirt?"	"You mean the one you wore when you dated the governor's son?"
"Harry, I'll drive!"	"Oh, great, the Mercedes!"
"Billy, your lunch money's on the mantel!"	"By your bowling trophy?"

By such fishing you learn how to get those around you to feed your affirmation/adulation need.

But after the dangling-angling technique comes the more sophisticated style of fishing. This affirmation game is called "trawling for the compliment." Trawling is different from mere angling. The angler has only a string, cork, and hook and catches primitively what he or she can. The trawler moves! He or she spends money to buy the necessary equipment and spares no cost to be sure the ego feeds. Trawlers move at high speed with stout line.

The businesswoman in a tailored suit with a leather portfolio, cash clip, and diamond ring is just off for a day's work, which she will get to as soon as she has her nails "reacryliced." From her designer frames to her Italian shoes, she glitters of expense. All she meets wish to know her and to be like her; her reputation precedes her Mercedes sports coupe and she walks with just the right speed—fast enough to say "I own Boardwalk and Park Place," and slow enough that anyone can approach her and say, "Aren't you Ms. Snodgrass, the inventor of the flexible marketing and management index?"

I will always remember Babs Bittendorf. At thirty-five, she Farrah Fawcetted her hair, fishnetted her slender legs, Izodded her shapely top, and crimped her eyelashes into upsweeping glory. Her Gucci shoes and Vanderbilt skirt adorned her body with the kind of allure that had everyone asking if there was anything they could get her. "Well . . ." she always hesitated, "I guess not!" The dolts who asked the question had already gotten her what she came to get: that hesitant question, "Is there anything I could get you?"

Babs was married to an early idolizer of hers. He had once been fascinated that her clothes were so little (usually just a little smaller than Babs). He adored her and showered her with gifts, despised her other idolaters, and quarreled with her flirtatious ways despite her insistence, "I have no idea what you are talking about—men hardly pay me any attention at all." He always responded, snapping at the trawl line, "You're a fool—the whole office is eating out of your hand." She would blush in denial as he told her once again that she ought to just open her eyes and look around.

I visited once with a handsome man who had married a Scandinavian heiress. She was a blonder version of Babs Bittendorf. Beautiful as a Swedish film star, she was an instant hit in coming to America and was so successful at trawling that she landed a job as a model with a leading ad agency. Her husband, who idolized her, confessed that she required more adulation than he could reasonably supply. "It is hard to be married to a beautiful heiress," he lamented.

It is hard to be the close associate of any trawler. There is in most affirmation the narcotic need for more. Finally, the search for affirmation is an intravenous transfer, siphoning life from mates or close friends to glut the greedy ego of the trawler. The high-speed trawler lives alone, trading fast-lane ego needs for the warmth and security he loses from family and friends. These close associates are pressed to supply him continually with all the compliments he wants.

Adulation is one step up from affirmation: Perhaps this is the main distinction between the trawler and the angler. The adulation need is symbolized by the trawler-devourer. Many public figures are consumed by the adulation need. Movie stars, concert artists, sportsmen, athletes are ravaged by the inner monster created by those who celebrate them.

On the Run for Approval

The new Narcissus is significantly different from his Greek prototype. The old Narcissus sat quietly at a pool to admire himself. The new Narcissus is an activist on the run for self-approval. Video religion has found a great many hungry gospel stars who are piteous evidence of this type. The Reverend Narcissus of Global Evangelistic Enterprises serves to illustrate. There is no egoism so all-consuming as that which marries Christ to Narcissus. Religious heroes turn every Sunday into Palm Sunday, as their admirers, sweeping as far as the satellite dishes may receive them, stand for the worldwide amen to all they say.

Who can deny they do it for Jesus? It was He to whom they originally gave their lives. When they first gave themselves to Jesus, they were nothing and "proud" to admit it. But this altruism came only at the beginning. With an imposing white marble headquarters building, it is hard to stand meekly in the shadow of Jesus. Thus they entered—all for Christ's sake, of course—the other mode. They cried out to those who attended them: "Sacrifice, and God will bless you. Deny and enjoy! Health, wealth, Jesus, and joy to all! A big howdy to all our new listeners on the Micronesia Network! Keep those cards and letters coming! Write today and receive our new Redemption Red Read-the-Bible-Through-in-a-Decade-Program. And don't forget our 'In the Steps of Paul' cruise. Now from all of us here at the Parousia Palace, may the God of big deals bless you real good."

Such superstars rarely face any negative evaluations of themselves. Since they will not make space for negative encounter, their egos grow with their empires in direct proportion.

Christ and Narcissus

I realize that to some extent all of us paint on Jesus the face we like best. Still, I am ever grateful that in my view of Him He is a Savior who does not teach self-sacrifice in ways that benefit himself. He does not urge camera crews in at the cross to photograph the great gift of Himself at just the proper angle with just the proper light. Having been followed by great crowds, He dies penniless and so utterly unknown (as Schweitzer discovered) that none of the Roman historians and thinkers of His day had ever heard of Him.

Jesus is, for all, the ultimate exposé. And in the light of His truth, we see the self-seeker Narcissus for what he is. Why is His "pennilessness" so important? Because in this way God still offers His only begotten as the Christ of the under-achiever. Narcissus is all *Fortune* magazine and *Wall Street Journal* stuff. He may, from time to time, feel a little setback, but he seldom knows the purgation of open shame.

Narcissus wins the seamless robe of Christ as he dices at the foot of the cross. He, of course, brags about it when his friends are collected, and even wears his winnings to the bar-racks banquet. But then Narcissus always wins. (And when he loses he never brings it up.) Winning is his destiny! Can he help it if the man who owned the robe was executed as a paragon of unappealing humility? The robe of the crucified low self-esteemer rightly came to him and is his.

Thus Jesus ever dies, and in His dying redeems.

Narcissus ever lives, and in his living grows smug.

Is this overpressing the categories of Narcissus and Jesus? We have no firm evidence that the actual dicer at the cross was an ardent lover of self. But we can at least say the "ap-parent winner" of Good Friday was the dicer and the "ap-parent loser" was the Son of God. Was Christ's robe the real prize of the cross gambler? Probably not—the real prize was likely the announcement of his win. To Narcissus it is the ac-colades that are imperative to him, and not his product. In truth, the accolades are his product!

Checkpoints for Keeping Narcissus at Bay

But how do you put a stop to your excessive need for affir-mation? You must make every need for affirmation pass cer-tain checkpoints.

Checkpoint A involves keeping a proper view of your product, even when under volleys of personal praise. Narcissism begins in slurring over the whole issue of excellence in product to grab the goody of self-esteem. Early in your career you give yourself to the perfecting of your product. But when people begin to "ooh" and "ahh" over what you produce, you often begin to drive for the "ooh" and the "ahh." Then your product becomes less important. Your hunger for approval may destroy the quality of your product altogether.

Nothing brings more joy to me than the release of a new book. Some fifteen times or so I have felt this wonderful exhilaration. Photos, reviews, speaking tours are the frosting on this most-delicious cake. Still, if you pin me down at these moments of self-surfeiting, I will freely confess that the frosting is mostly fluff, a meringue that cannot stand too much of the real heat in life. So I make myself ask the question, "What does all this hoopla really have to do with quality in life?" The finest books are not usually written in the whirl of speaking tours, but in lonely places like the Russian gulags, Bedford Jail, or Milton's study made black by blindness. Excellence falls easy victim to too much praise. If you want to be good at anything, you must not lose your way in the warm, sticky compliments, for flattery is often a great destroyer.

Checkpoint A requires a mental discipline. You must stay honest and avoid such phony denial as, "Oh, it was really nothing." You must read all compliments against the wideness of life. Even when the compliment is worthy, it is better still to cherish the product that inspired it.

The first checkpoint will provide a narrow sense of balance.

Within every maker is an honest and wholesome need for recognition. The artist is not so product-centered that he has no need to hang his work for others to see. He paints pictures to be hung and observed. The recognition that comes to him will not keep the good artist from painting; it will rather incite him to produce an even better painting in the future.

Likewise, praise becomes your incentive to more product and the criticism becomes your guide to change and improvement. You may enjoy the limelight, but this does not make you a Narcissus. You are not a Narcissus until your esteem paralyzes you with such joy that the paralysis stops your production or causes you to slur over quality in your race to gain applause.

Checkpoint B is closely coupled with Checkpoint A in that it stresses your way back to the real world. Checkpoint B says that adulation is most frequently given by those who know you least. The people who know you best no longer gape when you enter the room. *Checkpoint B is your acceptance of life among those who know you well and therefore affirm you least.* You must not allow yourself to swim in any sea of approval for too long. Forcing yourself to say no to the next speaking tour or to reject a healthy advance from a new publisher may be step one. Then you must enter the world of real people where you have to live and produce.

This real world for me has always been the church I pastor. I have been there for twenty years. After that length of time, a sermon that might bring furious "amens" on a speaking tour is only passively observed. Still, my church is my arena of realistic living. Nobody there long stops to celebrate my product for here they are all making products of their own. Here, at the back door of my life, I discover that the most valid role I may play as a minister is to affirm their product and create in them a sense of worth. To see an old man or a child trying to pick at the oysters of life for some pearl of meaning makes me want to see them as Christ sees them. If I can help them stand a little straighter or believe in themselves in the present heaviness of life, my life will have served them well.

The noncelebrative world of plain old home is the sure cure for egomania. The superstars and limelighters of this world have not been known to have the most stable marriages. I suspect that a large factor in the superstar divorce rate has to do with the fact that their homes are less affirming than their celebrity-hyped fan clubs.

The mates of celebrities are often at a loss to know how to keep the adulation of the fan club alive in the workaday world. The person whose personal career is star-studded should never lay upon his loved ones the burden of keeping

the flashbulbs popping between performances. The lime-
lighter should welcome home as the place where he takes his
own turn at building others' self-esteem. It's their turn! They
have often waited in the wings while his career was celebrated.

At this point, you may discover whether or not you are a
Narcissus. Can you live without your mirror? The mirror of
Narcissus is the stagestruck arena of glorious affirmation. But
your mirror as a real person is those relationships of life that
are too close to celebrate you constantly. The mirror of the
adjusted, integrated person says loud and clear: "Here I
am—reflected in the ordinary days of growing older in my responsibility of genuinely caring for others." In short, the issue
boils down to this: Who you are when you are celebrated
may be nothing but helium ego. But who you are when life is
too ordinary to celebrate you is who you really are.

The noncelebrating world is always the back door. At the
front door is the best paint, the wrought iron, the open invi-
tation to adore you. But at the back door is the old carpet, the
dog run, the litter box, the trash service. Here you remember
that you are called to affirm someone other than yourself.
The excellence of your product may one day bring some
long-awaited flood of esteem, but for now it is enough that
you do the best that you can at whatever you conceive your
product to be; at the same time you create for others of your
closest acquaintances the right to produce something too.

*Checkpoint C for expanding egos consists of your inviolate
principles.* There are certain principles that you cannot run
past in your need to succeed. Their power over you may be
set against Narcissus in your life. An example from the arts
occurs in the film *Chariots of Fire.* The Scot, Eric Liddell,
wants so very much to be an Olympiad medal winner. But he
also has an obligation to honor the Sabbath. In the large
Olympic world, his personal convictions seem such a little
thing. But winning to him is far less important than principles, and so he refuses to run on the Sabbath. The point is
made in the film that "God honors those who honor Him."
Still, you need to remember that the honors are not always as

automatic or visible as they appear in the film. Even so, your principles should always keep your self-serving ego in check.

One of the power insinuations of the Book of Job is that everyone has a price. Satan's wager in this stirring drama is that under proper pressure and for the proper price everyone will sell out. The point is made by the end of the book that not everyone will sell—Job would not! Still, Satan finds many takers when his stakes are high and the pressures of self-aggrandizement are applied.

Principles get abandoned for many reasons. The hunger for power, security, comfort: All are major appetites that can lure you into compromise. These drives are narcissistic to the core.

But there are other more subtle influences. Fatigue! Sometimes in the overlong pursuit of truth, you grow tired and fatigue can lead you to self-doubt and vacant cynicism. It can lead to the same kind of anger that caused Moses (after incessant implacable criticism) to smite the rock. Moses was tired! But Moses' sin against his principles was costly. Fatigue can be a destroyer of your will and thus serve in the erosion of your principles. Here you must be careful, for your character itself is the gift of your principles.

Let Narcissus take note: Fatigued or not, the good man never tires in his defense of the good. The principle that holds your character is in reality not for sale.

I have a good friend who was tempted to mischief in a foreign city: He was encouraged by a friend to go ahead and participate in the evil. "No one would ever know—do it—enjoy!" "That is not quite right," said my friend. "I would know and God would know and we would both stand as a pair of judges over my action."

Checkpoint D is self-denial. You must allow Jesus' words to remind you that nothing has lasting value that is performed merely in your own interest. "Deny yourself," said Jesus, "and take up your cross, and then you can be my disciple" (*see* Luke 9:23). Self-denial is not a grand decision that you make once and for all. Self-denial is a daily and oft painful choice you must make. It is Rosa Parks during the Montgomery bus boycott, walking a long distance across the city to say to Montgomery, "My feets gits tired," but there is, after all, something more important than my personal comfort. Self-denial is Gandhi fasting to the edge of death to reconcile Moslems and Hindus. Self-denial is Jesus holding our needs in His heart saying to His Father, "This cup, which the Father has given me, shall I not drink it?—What shall I say, Father, save me from this hour? But for this cause am I come to this hour" (*see* John 12:27).

Your own self-exaltation will in time give you the soul of Narcissus. To be a better soul, you must make self-denial a daily practice. The word *daily* must become as big a word as the cross. Intermittent denial will do you no good. Between the times you take it up, your ego can rise and serve itself to your own undoing. When intermittent gets too much "inter" between the "mittents," your spiritual discipline gets shoddy.

You can manage it all by resolving the whole issue of your willingness to be crucified with Christ. In the palm of your left hand at approximately the place where Saint Francis experienced the stigmata, write Romans 6:11, that you "have reckoned ourselves dead to all personal ambition but remain alive in Christ." In the palm of your right hand, write Galatians 2:20, that you are "crucified with Christ, nevertheless you live." Crucified men may on the very cross celebrate the great cause that put them there, but the cross is not a place you might voluntarily choose for profit or personal gain. Once you have assigned such stigmata to your own hands, the voluntary crucifixion of yourself will have dealt with Narcissus.

Self-crucifixion is usually not very visible, even though it requires the utmost in discipline. Your whole life, excellently lived, will be composed of small but important denials. Rosa Parks will illustrate. See her trudging across Montgomery on a hot day, voluntarily taking the harder way. While empty city buses roar by her, she smiles, for she has acted on principles. She has reined down hard on her need to take the easy way. Walt Whitman said, if you want me, look for me beneath the soles of your feet, for that is where you will find me.

The final checkpoint—*Checkpoint E—is the principle of abandonment.* Here and there in life you must give up your product because some great need intersects your own dreams and desires. Paul was interrupted on the road to Damascus midpoint in his own career. Narcissus was slain, and the old Paul was lost to one whose new desire grew so overwhelmingly powerful that his old dreams were completely abandoned.

Jesus said, "He who loves his life shall lose it" (*see* John 12:25). Here was one of His most direct confrontations with Narcissus. You must let go. Relinquish. Abandon. Narcissus is a liar. You may not hold the good things of life by grasping.

Conclusion

Don't forget that what we have just dealt with are checkpoints. We have done this to hold Narcissus at bay. We are not, in these brief pages, suggesting asceticism. Balance is the key. God ordered Adam to be fruitful: God put him in Eden "to work it and take care of it" (Genesis 2:15 NIV), that is, to produce. Man is a maker who wants to create that which speaks of excellence.

Perhaps the final resolution will come by understanding that you must model your life after Christ and not some other image of power, affluence, or scholarship. You can then produce in such a way as to say, "I am His, and He has created me, like Himself, to make and enjoy what I make." Thinking well of yourself is important to you. It is also important to God. Producing beautiful things produces beautiful lives and fuels your confidence.

9

Losing
Without
Being
a Loser

The man recovered of the bite,
The dog it was that died.
> Oliver Goldsmith, "Elegy on a Mad Dog"

I wouldn't join any club that would have me as a member.
> Groucho Marx

Champions are pioneers, and pioneers get shot at.
> Thomas J. Peters and Robert H.
> Waterman, Jr., *In Search of Excellence*

Winning is a matter of focus and discipline. Losing happens because we misjudge the race or fail to prepare adequately or do not struggle to win. Losing often occurs simply because we do not focus on winning.

Consider the Wallendas. Karl Wallenda fell to his death in 1978. This great aerialist, who had spent his life in the airy void, failed to negotiate a high wire in San Juan, Puerto Rico. His wife later recalled: "All Karl thought about for three straight months prior to it [the accident] was *falling*. It was the first time he'd ever thought about that, and it seemed to me that he put all his energies into *not falling* rather than walking the tightrope." Mrs. Wallenda, an aerialist herself, said that in the insecurity that marked her husband's final days, he even began checking the guy wires himself to make sure they were secure. He had never done that before—not once during his entire career.[1] Losing often results from the failure to focus on winning.

Explaining all losses on the basis of the "Wallenda factor" is oversimplistic, for many who do focus on winning lose. And the critical question for self-esteem asks, do losses make losers?

The Wallenda factor occurs when the innate self and the quantum self lose their harmony. The innate self questions and doubts that the quantum self will be able to maintain the production of that product which brought it outer esteem and thus a feeling of inner worth as well. Now this inner-outer harmony becomes jangled by inner doubt.

Ernest Hemingway in a short story tells of a trio of soldiers who crucify Jesus and then stop by a tavern after the execution to have a drink. Two of them are more or less impressed with Jesus at His hour of dying, but one of the soldiers is shaken by what he has seen. This misty-eyed soldier sees himself as somehow corrupted by his participation in the crucifixion. He keeps shaking his head and saying, "He sure looked good in there today . . . He sure looked good in there today."[2]

It is not just the dying of Christ that is important. It is also important that Jesus really did "look good in there." By the secular, objective standards of the day, Jesus seemed as much a loser as any executed criminal. Yet the majesty of Good Friday is that while Jesus appeared to lose, He was clearly no loser.

Crosses were not unique to Jesus. They were common dying places in Jesus' time, and are, in a broader sense, frequent living ordeals in our own day. You may have already discovered that life can sometimes dump such severe hurt upon you that you will not be able to win. Christ's cross should remind you that your pain or loss is common to humanity.

All your feelings of being a loser are couched in the innate self. Your quantum self is there and functioning and still gaining for you a great deal of outer esteem. But your innate self will no longer let this outer product esteem be translated into positive feelings of self-esteem. In the last chapter I will deal with the damaged self. For now, let me assume that most of your feelings of losing are not because your ego is damaged but because your innate self and quantum self are not accurately communicating the nature of your wins and losses.

What you produce furnishes you with self-esteem and keeps you from seeing yourself a loser. We are all motivated to buy books—and there are many—on winning in life, but none are printed on how to lose. My high school motto spoke of "modesty in victory and an unconquerable spirit in defeat." The motto really translated, "Lose without being a loser!" You may find that losing without feeling yourself a loser is as hard as winning without overcelebrating. Muhammad Ali was an overcelebrator who consistently referred to himself as "the greatest." One prominent evangelical Christian was being interviewed by a satirical magazine. This notable interviewee immodestly said of himself, "I had a rising and promising film career," to which the interviewer said, "Other people are supposed to say you have a rising and promising film career."[3]

If you are like most, you would rather hear others call you a winner than to call yourself one. And conversely, you would rather call yourself a loser than have others do so. It is important to remember that about 50 percent of your life contests will end in losing. It is possible to push those percentages here and there, but for the most part, on the day you die you will be batting about .500. Remembering that you are going to miss every other ball you swing at makes it easier to continue swinging and retain your self-respect.

The Fifty-Fifty Principle

Fifty-fifty becomes your percentage of peace. Therefore, you will have to resist the notion that you ought always to win. You have been told that winning is not merely important, it is all-important. Losing is not so much a shame as it is average. The word *loser* by popular definition is not one who loses but one who is socially inept and not worthy of place. The connotation of the word *loser* is that of a person who finishes last regularly and is therefore disgusting.

Average carries a different connotation. The average is the person who just doesn't come in first. But average, even as a middle position, is not considered to be desirable. Average is the best of the worst and the worst of the best. There is such an ambiguity in being average that everyone hesitates to say, "I lose some."

Since winning is well understood, perhaps it needs no special definition. Winning is having your product judged the best in any contest or comparison, regardless of the number of entries. To win is to have your product spoken of in the best possible way. The beauty queen is the most comely of all the entries. The chess champion is he who can checkmate all who come against him. The roses go to the Derby champ. Winning is always a positive word, stated in a positive way. The beauty queen is always said to be the most beautiful and not the least ugly. The chess champion is the best, not the least poor; the Derby winner is fastest not the least slow. But when it comes to losers, they are always spoken of in the negative. Since winning or losing occurs in all lives, the entire issue of being winners or losers is a matter of your own mindset.

Earl Wilson confesses: "I was amazed the first time I heard one of my sons refer to himself as a loser. . . . As I questioned him, I realized he had developed this view from a few isolated failures."[4] The person who says, "I'm a loser," is so locked in self-pity he becomes a momentary liar. Such a statement seems to say, "I customarily lose." At most, the self-proclaimed loser is only a half-time loser. The other half of the time he wins.

Winning and losing is the stuff of life. Winners may win more than they lose, but only in certain areas where their training and discipline make them winners. For instance, I once played a professional football player and beat him at racquetball. Racquetball was not his customary arena of winning. He did not feel bad being a loser at racquetball because he did not have the same need to win at this game that he did at football. Fortunately he did not ask me to play against him in football.

Remember: Nobody is a winner in every area and nobody remains a lifetime winner in any area. Once you accept the fifty-fifty principle, you will enjoy a more consistent self-esteem. Still, what is to be said of those for whom even infrequent loss spells damage? The ones who cannot stand any losing? If the issue of being the best in every area is all-important to your self-esteem, you will not be able to lose any contest without seeing yourself as a loser. If you have such self-esteem problems, you need to examine these seven blessings of losing.

The Seven Blessings of Losing

Losing, first of all, can help you understand what life is really like. There is a narcotic effect in always winning that can lead you to the delusion that all that matters is winning. "Winning isn't everything; it is the only thing," said Vince Lombardi, the originator of the self-confidence cliché "Show me a good loser and I'll show you a loser."

I could not disagree more with Lombardi. Show *me* a good loser and I'll show you a person who can negotiate the nasty turns of life and keep a self-view adequate to keep going. The more seriously you take the doctrine of winning, the more devastating becomes the psychology of the crash. Pain and glory come bound together in life. It is a matter of critical adjustment for you to be able to lose and to keep standing after the loss. Why is standing so important? It's your salvation as a "sometimes loser." But remember, a good loser is not an "every time" loser.

A *second blessing of losing is that loss makes us approachable.* Constant winning fosters the narcissism we discussed in the last chapter. Thomas à Kempis said:

> It is good that people sometimes misunderstand us, that they have a poor opinion of us even when our intentions are good. Such experiences lead us toward humility and protect us from conceit. Under trying circumstances we seek God all the more. Our inner life grows stronger when we are outwardly condemned.[5]

How true! It is important for you to lose because consistent winning seldom fosters approachability. Arrogance is the most likely product of the regular win. Older men often have eyes that see clearer because they have so often been washed with the tears of failure. Young winners rarely make good counselors, for only those who lose can teach others how to stand in loss.

A *third blessing of losing is the perception of illusion.* Your losing can help you see through the misty now of shallow positivism. Have you ever wondered, "What spawns the American positivist doctrine that everyone can win?" Positivism is not born in Somalia, where refugees without any land or hope of employment can "take charge of their lives" and "succeed." The poverty of the Third World will not allow its dreamless gutter sleepers the remote consideration of being head of a company.

It is an illusion to believe that everyone in the world can wind up rich. Many will have to live a life that conquers their spirit, regardless of the strength of their positive mental attitude. But it is better to take life as it comes than to sugarcoat reality with a pretense of continuous victory.

Fourth, losing also teaches us that life is of value even when we are not winning. I sat with a man whose depressive wife had just committed suicide. Despair had sifted all through his sense of confidence in himself and his ability to make any headway against his uncertain future. "Still," he said, "as bleak as life is, I could never kill myself [as his wife had just done]; there is too much worth living for."

If I count those instances when "Jesus wept," there are four. These are not positive moments in the Savior's life, but His own need to be in existence with us seems to say that even when life seems not worth living, it still is. Jesus' tears are one of His powerful lessons that there is meaning in spite of loss.

God never bails out in the darkness. You may experience times when you doubt that God is there. At such times you may feel God is an ogre for sending the trial. You are surrounded by darkness and you don't know why. If you could see reasons for the darkness, it would leave you too much knowing and too little trusting. Emilie Griffin wrote, ". . . our God is not playing tricks. He doesn't set traps like some Olympian practical joker of a deity. Instead, the darkness he sends is so real that you can't see your hand in front of your face. So real that you can't suspect it has been sent as a gift."[6] Such darkness is beyond your analysis. Like the Savior, you may want to cry, "My God, my God, why hast thou forsaken me?" (Matthew 27:46 KJV). He may not answer you that the darkness is only for a while. In fact, He sometimes doesn't seem to answer you at all.

Still, all is not loss: Jesus is proof that an overwhelming victory waits on our patience. All temporary loss can be sustained with meaning in anticipation of that coming victory. Even positivists believe in temporary loss. Their view of temporary means but a loss in some portion of life. Temporary to Jesus, however, might mean the whole of life. "Nothing is profited to gain (temporarily) the whole world and lose (permanently) our own souls," said Jesus (*see* Matthew 16:26).

Fifth, losing provides the contrast against which your winning can be defined. You can never know what winning is unless you have experienced some losing here and there to give it definition. It is incredible that certain promoters see success without any failure to be everybody's lot in life. How blind! If everybody were successful, there would be no pall of failure to teach us what success is.

The sixth blessing of losing is perceiving the wealth hidden in simple things. It takes more and more to titillate and fascinate the rich. The poor learn the celebration of the ordinary. There is an old popular song that testifies, "The best things in life are free." There is something in poverty and loss that whets perception and sees the victory that wealth cannot. No wonder Jesus said, "Consider the lilies of the field; they toil not neither do they spin, yet Solomon in all his glory was not arrayed like one of these" (*see* Matthew 6:28, 29).

But the seventh and final blessing of losing is that losing is the foundation of need. When you win, you need no one but yourself, but when you lose you become dependent on others. "There is," says Louis Evely, "a great fraternity of the poor." The poor have need of each other. When failure comes you are in need. When you need you will reach out. When you can no longer boast your self-sufficiency, you are made recipients of that great love that others must extend to all of us. Such love comes from those who can understand your loss and pain, for they too have faced it.

But what are the ways that losing most relates to your product and your evaluation of it? Losing can teach you very quickly which of your products are enduring. Many are they who have had to discover that fortune, fame, and winning itself are transient.

You also would learn in such moments that a strong selfview can never derive from shallow popular viewpoints that see no value in losing. At any moment of losing, you must quickly come to a stronger viewpoint of what it means to be measured by a standard that individually allows you to think well of yourself, even when your product has diminished or found no esteem in the success-oriented world around you.

Losing to Win

Most of my years I have been the pastor of a moderately affluent, suburban congregation. Many of these own-your-own-home-and-two-cars Americans are able to buy books and attend seminars on how to have a full and meaningful life. Success is so important to many of them that they have given their lives to its pursuit. Still, I have not found these—even though they were "Christians"—altogether happy.

I have known missionaries who—unlike my congregation—could not measure their "product" in stocks, bonds, chattel, or other securities. Still, their sense of product was enduring. Their lives themselves became the expression of that product. Each day, each hour, every year was an offering to Christ. In the giving of their lives, they grew older. The years stole their vitality and, finally conquered by pain and hurt, they passed into the presence of Christ. But it was not a dull passing. There was a brightness of eye that proclaimed, "I gave my life for something that really mattered." Most of these might have been considered losers by the financial, multi-ulcered achievers of our day. But these apparent losers were made winners by their abundant sense of enduring product.

I have a friend named Mike Milliton who demonstrates the point. After a brilliant military career, Mike entered Harvard law school. His "cum laude" graduation set him immediately into a successful practice. He was on the way to a big home and a well-earned reputation as a trial lawyer.

Still, law left him feeling as though he was only a well-paid referee at courthouse contests over penny-ante issues where the stakes were much higher than the issues. Ultimately, Mike decided to leave his practice and enter an Episcopal seminary. Earning a second "cum laude" degree, this time in theology, he moved his family to Central America where he even now serves as a missionary. The torrid and yet monsoon climate nearer the equator has brought him much sickness. He has, from time to time, been put to bed for weeks to deal with chronic hepatitis. The Indians he chose to serve spoke a language for which he could find no adult teacher. The housing in the jungle village is inadequate.

Have all these circumstances led him to secondary considerations? Hardly. "This is really living!" he exulted recently in my presence. "My life at last has meaning!"

The theology of the evangelical church has often led us to see ourselves as losers. Even men like Mike Milliton have been taught to despise their sacrifice because they are after all only sinners. Earl Wilson speaks of a nineteen-year-old girl named Joan. Most people who knew her considered her intelligent and pretty. But Joan had almost no good feelings about herself. As a child, Joan had been told by her parents a thousand times, "Remember, Joan, there is nothing good in you. God is the only person who is good."

Joan became more self-condemning. In reaching out to believe in herself, on one occasion she went to hear a religious speaker on campus. He thundered out the same put-down theology of her parents. While she sat listening, desperately wanting to believe in herself, this preacher cried against all of her hopes: "You will never have peace of mind until you accept the fact that you are totally rotten. Nothing in you is good. You must die to yourself. You must recognize that you are a worm."[7] The theology of the evangelical church has often contributed to fostering the loser syndrome among those it sought to bring to Christ. Often, as it sought to bring joy to its converts, it taught them to see themselves as losers, completely worthless in the sight of God, and thus their own.

The tragedy of worm theology is that it is communicated at the deepest levels of the psyche—the very heart of the innate self. Unless its utter negativity is dislodged, all that the quantum self achieves in terms of product is put down as insignificant. Some evangelicals couple with this negative inner thinking a terrible put-down of all outer achievement. The phrase "It'll burn!" is a statement used by superspiritual zealots to say that nothing we do will matter in light of eternity unless it is "spiritual." One such man told me the works of Michelangelo were trash and would perish when God destroyed the world. Michelangelo's art is, after 400 years, a part of the artist's quantum definition, and yet the whole productive self is worthless in relation to the only self that matters, say such spiritual zealots: the innate self.

Seeing Our Losses in Perspective

To complete this chapter, we must interpret this whole issue of loss—loss that can lead you to believe you are a loser. How do you deal with feelings of loss? The question which can clarify is: Is a loss really a loss? If it is not, then you can scarely be a loser. This sounds like double-talk, yet it is all a matter of how you view your loss. There are four ways of seeing your losses in perspective. *In the first place you need to ask: Was your loss really a loss or a win in disguise?*

Some years ago our landlord evicted us from the house we had rented for six years. He had decided to sell the house without telling us and, as soon as he found a buyer, he gave us notice that we had to move. We felt a desperate sense of disinheritance. We were frantic in our search for an apartment, since we had been living in one of the few rental houses available in our part of the city.

I called a friend of mine in real estate who asked me, "Have you considered buying your own home?" I had not. I explained to him that the church we pastored was small and could ill afford to pay us a living wage. Therefore we could not buy. "Don't be so sure," he counseled. He was a devious and glorious friend. He not only had a particular home in mind, but he planned to give us his selling commission, which was the two thousand dollars we needed to make the down payment. Soon our feelings of loss turned to utter win. We lived in our own home for the first time in our lives and were happier than we had ever been. What appeared to be losing was winning in disguise.

A second look at ways of seeing your losses in perspective is simply to wait and see. There is a scene in the film *Force 10 From Navarrone* where a demolitions team has just set off a blast in the heart of a great dam in the hope of demolishing the dam and the bridge before it, thus halting the movement of enemy troops across the bridge. Once the dam explosion had settled, however, nothing moved. The explosion was a failure.

But the demolitions man, when accused of failing, said, "Wait and see." The inner structure of the dam sprang a leak, the leaks turned from drops to spurts, from spurts to gushers, and at last from gushers to volleys of water pressured by the silent depths. Soon the dam shot explosions of water from a dozen orifices and these exploded, destroying both the dam and the bridge before it. Losses so often require a wait and see attitude to display what they really are.

A third look at whether losing really is such is to ask whether this loss is from our viewpoint or from all viewpoints. When my son was old enough to play tennis, we began playing. He played for years, losing a thousand matches. But the inevitable day came, in his sixteenth year, when he soundly defeated me. It was a loss—but not for him. And in a sense, his joy at winning was so great that it unconsciously swept me into joy as well.

Finally, seeing our losses in perspective means that losing must be measured against the whole picture. Indeed, it is a wise person who can continue to integrate losing and winning in such a way as to remember that the war is not the battle. Pearl Harbor was a great loss to us! But it was the Japanese who ultimately surrendered. You can lose in life without being losers. The best part of service to any person is to see how you might use the simple tool of encouragement to remind them that few losses are irreparable, and no single loss makes anyone a loser.

An IBM luminary had to counsel a young executive who, in a forthright but risky business deal, had lost the company ten million dollars. When the young executive was called into the head office to give account, he said, "I suppose you'll be wanting my resignation." To which Thomas J. Watson, IBM's founder, replied, "You can't be serious. We've just spent ten million educating you!"[8]

Such affirmations at the zero hour are turning points in

self-esteem. Perhaps this kind of affirmation is hiding in the parable of the prodigal son. Having just botched the family fortune, he cries to his father, "Father, you couldn't possibly want me any longer as a son . . . could you?"

"Son, I've got an entire inheritance invested in you . . . could we start again . . . please?"

Conclusion

Perhaps this is why grace is the great gift to this world. In grace we are reinstated in great esteem. The loser awaits transformation. The continual power of acceptance and affirmation melts the negative self-image and reshapes it into a remarkable person who believes in God and self. In short, it puts faith and product in touch with each other—the innate believing self and the outer quantum self are joined in the wholeness of a genuine self-esteem. This double faith is the parent of meaning and product.

10

Repairing the Damaged Self

Raised without love, children come to believe themselves unlovable.

M. Scott Peck, *People of the Lie*

When, in disgrace with Fortune and men's eyes,
I all alone weep my outcast state,
. . . .
Wishing me like to one more rich in hope,
Featur'd like him, like him with friends possess'd,
Desiring this man's art and that man's scope. . . .

William Shakespeare

When I have ceased to break my wings
Against the faultiness of things,
And learned that compromises wait
Behind each hardly opened gate,
When I can look Life in the eyes,
Grown calm and very coldly wise,
Life will have given me the Truth,
And taken in exchange—my youth.

Sara Teasdale, "Wisdom"

Some years ago a child was discovered who had been reared in the wilderness, Tarzan fashion, by wolves. The child could perform superhuman physical feats, but had little awareness of herself as a "self"! Her inability to see herself as a whole person resulted from the absence of real community in her childhood. This kind of child is rare, but think for a moment of all who live with a dwarfed concept of themselves because their environment has provided them too little reflection and support. You do not have to be raised by wolves to know that the harsh brutality of life can damage your self-perception.

It is normal for us to want to think well of ourselves. The fairy tale *Snow White* sets the tone for the struggle. The wicked queen in arrogance has one neurotic compulsion as she faces her all-affirming mirror. The answer to "Mirror, mirror on the wall, who's the fairest of them all?" is asked out of a narcissistic compulsion. She simply can't stand to be second. We may ask ourselves this question all our lives. Unlike the wicked queen, we do not have to hear the mirror say we are "the fairest one of all," but we would like to hear it say, "Congratulations, you're in the top ten." We all want to place in life.

This wonderful "magic" mirror performs two miracles. It allows us to stand outside ourselves and gain perspective. It also provides us a comparative feedback in our social standings. We would like to get free of the prison of our bodies so we could see ourselves in some mirror of comparison. Then we could measure how well we really do compete in our world.

Symptoms of the Damage

It is normal to want to think well of ourselves. If we cannot, our psyche has been damaged. The undamaged self can nearly always find reasons to congratulate itself. But the damaged self always approaches the magic mirror in fear. It hesitates to ask the mirror, "How do I place? How am I surviving in a world of adjusted people? How am I really doing?" It fears any dialogue with the mirror of self-evaluation for fear of being put on hold while the mirror snickers.

"What's the use?" The damaged self laments. "I know I'm not the fairest one of all. I don't even count. I can't place. I hate myself."

There are many indicators of ego damage. Damaged egos are unable to cope with things they ought to be able to manage. The rough spots of life that others handle with some ease leave the damaged self disoriented and confused.

The damaged self, finding itself unable to cope, seizes upon an accommodation to life rather than struggling with the management of life. Withdrawal becomes its way of dealing with challenge. The confrontation of threatening circumstances is not seen as within its capabilities. Instead of finding and relating to other celebrants of life, the damaged self has an inner urge to identify with other noncombatants. The damaged ones commiserate together: "I had that same trouble once, dearie, and I was just as miserable as you are."

Misery in the damaged self is a pleasure all its own. Dostoyevsky, in his *Notes from Underground,* reminds us that the groans of the sufferer of a toothache are an expression of sheer pleasure. If the groans were not pleasurable the sufferer would cease groaning: "He realizes that even the audience for which he is performing, even his own family, are sick of listening to him, they don't believe a word of it, and they know in their hearts that he could very well groan in another, simpler fashion, without roulades and flourishes, and is merely indulging himself out of spite and ill humour."[1] Loud, overt misery is often pleasure to the damaged self. It is a way to call forth an audience from the world of those who are winning.

These selves who are badly damaged can trump up sympathy for their condition that is completely irrational. Studs Terkel tells of such a man.

> Nothing terrible happened to Hanson, other than a crying jag one Saturday afternoon. He had had a few. What was the trouble? I asked him.
>
> "My father died."

There were soft, fumbled, solicitous murmurs and silence. My mother, passing by, reached in under the rolltop desk and withdrew a pint. She uncorked it, set it down by the Swede and patted his shoulder.

"When did it happen?" I asked.

"Thirty years ago," he blubbered.

My mother, without missing a beat, corked the bottle and replaced it in the rolltop desk.[2]

Such misery gives birth to a camaraderie of commiseration. It rehearses little ills for years. Its creed, in some sense, is, "Let's just groan together. We will both feel better!" We had a neighbor once who majored in the ministry of commiseration. Whatever ill we came upon, she had already experienced: kidney infections, tonsillitis, thinning hair! We found her constant identification with our woes a little too regular.

This useless kind of identification only seeks to legitimize your own depression.

Noncopers, Depressives, and Comics

Depression is a symptom of the noncoper. Depression is the unwelcome soul guest who says the innate self is under the heavy heel of a burdensome psychology. No matter the quality of the quantum self and its lavish outer esteem. No real headway can be made toward inner peace. Self-esteem is usually not possible for those walled in by depression, but self-concern is. Those who cope with depressives continually and unsuccessfully have to admit they are among the most selfish on earth. They cannot be free of their woeful entanglement in their own affairs to show even an instant of concern elsewhere.

Their selfishness brings them little joy. It all but eliminates their sense of accomplishment and product. Counselors usually try to instruct the hurting to get out in the world again and get busy. The idea is that busyness prohibits depression from becoming too burdensome to manage. Depression feeds on idle thought and time. But it wallows masochistically in the tearful space it makes for itself.

The perpetual comic, like the depressive, also walls himself off from the burdensome need to succeed. Joke by joke, he uses laughter to convince himself he still has all the world's attention, while he actually holds little of the world's admiration. Frequently, those who have to deal with a degenerative or terminal disease play the clown to avoid the burden of their days. They trump up a levity they usually do not feel. Their flamboyant quantum self is light-years distant from their hollow innate self. With humor they keep them widely separate.

The comic is so often one whose low self-esteem and limited sense of product keep him from being all he might. The continual comic and the continual depressive both shut out reality. So, for that matter, it is with the constant cynic.

The Darkened Judgment of the Damaged Self

These are all damaged selves. The question is, what are the behavior patterns of these egos maimed by the brutality of life? The damaged self is not one that does not *want* to think well of itself; rather it is one that *cannot* think well of itself. The troubles with the damaged self are deep. This self lives underneath a cyclical curse. The things that damaged the self in the first place are the very things that return to it time and time again to keep it from healing.

Judith Deem Dupree wrote in "Tangent" these magnificent words:

> *Your life begins*
> *Somewhere beyond*
> *   my radius.*
> *I scour my scuffed*
> *   circumference*
> *For signs of you. . . .*
> . . . .
> *Held fast, again,*
> *   at last,*
> *By who I am.*[3]

The negative image of self cannot allow us the freedom to be healed. What it might become is always tied to what it is.

But does this have to be? Can we be more than we are?

What we are is always potential. That is why in the closing pages of this book I now turn to deal with God's view of the damaged self. The God view of who we are is always circumvented by a heavy darkness. This darkness separates how God sees us from how we see ourselves. The darkness is common to all injured egos. The injured self may think it sees correctly; but its vision is distorted.

Remember in Hugo's *The Hunchback of Notre Dame* what Quasimodo said to Esmeralda? "Yes . . . this is how I'm made. It's horrible, isn't it? And you're so beautiful!"[4] Now the issue for Quasimodo was, what am I really like? Quasimodo's ugliness was real, but his total compassion made him the hero of Hugo's imagination. He had acquired a sense of worthlessness from the thousand condemning assessments of children and peasants who hooted and jeered his twisted form. Finally he had accepted their assessment of himself.

It is hard to stand against others' dark opinions of who we are. It seems inevitable that Quasimodo finally saw himself only as he was seen. No longer could he stand outside the darkness of human judgment and see himself in brighter light.

But where does this darkened judgment begin? I think it begins subliminally in our hearts and minds as we overreact to the unkind feedback we encounter. In the early pages of this book we spoke of the "athletic ideal" against which we measure our own physical appearance in a culture that bases so much on physical appearance.

So naturally one of the things we need to do is separate the authenticity of our selves from the physical state of ourselves. We are so much more than body size or physical appearance. Buckminster Fuller confesses that the true "me" operates on another deeper level of self-awareness. At seventy-eight, Buckminster Fuller had lost seventy pounds and deliberated what really was lost. "The seventy pounds I got rid of was ten times the flesh-and-bone inventory at which I had weighed in, in 1895.

"I am certain that I am not the avoirdupois of the most recent meals I have eaten, some of which will become my hair, only to be cut off twice a month. This lost seventy pounds of organic chemistry obviously wasn't 'me,' nor are any of the remaining presently associated atoms 'me.' "[5] The self is always more than our physical size or organic definition.

When I was a boy the cultural hero was that superachiever from the planet Krypton. Even in his reporter's getup he looked better than I did. By the time I was fourteen years of age I was 6 feet 2 inches, spiraling up out of adolescence. I weighed just over 100 pounds. Each time I went to the beach I was reminded that I looked like an X ray in a bathing suit.

Gym class was worse than the beach because it came so regularly. I have long felt that public-school gymnasiums are a kind of violence for the thin and shy. I found myself hating the class where the more mesomorphic types entered the locker room strutting with pride while I picked locker number 99 in the distant corner, out of the way and out of the light. Being chosen last for every athletic team contest left me feeling last all through school. I was good at Latin grammar, but that sort of skill held little interest in an Oklahoma high school in the fifties.

Those classes were not set up to make me contemptuous of myself. That happened when I overvalued the assessment of my peers. It took me years to get over my self-recriminating feelings. I rehearsed them continually in the day-by-day hatred I felt for the class we called simply "gym."

These same things occur in children's lives today. Little boys play with plastic replicas of the "Incredible Hulk" or one of the superheroes. All of these are well-muscled miniature mannequins that are powerful, primitive, savage, and macho. But these little herculean figures are not merely toys. They are the strong foundations of fantasies—dream fodder for that which becomes the unspoken standard for every thin-chested child. But what happens when the chubby baby has elongated into an adolescent scarecrow, feeling strangely betrayed by life? At 6 feet 2 inches and 113 pounds, the Halloween-door-hanger teenager will have to admit, "Incredible Hulk, I am not." Low self-esteem then begins to move into his quiet moments.

Little girls do not play with the GI Joe dolls, but allow themselves a dreaming identity with Barbie dolls. Their absorption in the fantasy world of Ken and Barbie costs their parents a fortune in tiny clothes. But what has been equally costly for many a young girl is the keeping of those shapely dolls only to discover that her early adolescent figure falls far short of the busty, luscious dolls of her prepuberty fascination.

I remember an incident in the life of one of the young teenage girls in our congregation. This Barbie-owning adolescent was a little lankier and thinner than she would have liked to be. One day when she had just put on a bathing suit that would have been revealing (if there had been anything to reveal), her brother looked at her thirteen-year-old-bust and called her "flatso." She broke into tears at this and left the room. Of course the parents chided her brother for throttling her self-esteem. But what had really strangled her self-esteem? Had her years of playing with all those miniature, supershaped Miss Americas taken their toll on her view of herself—the Barbie doll she had not become by age thirteen?

In the cases cited above, the plastic icons of the super-heroes and heroines before adolescence is not enough to damage an underdeveloped self, if the normal channels of affirmation and production remain in good shape. But if one couples these unachieved ideals with such things as crushing parental authority or too little affirmation, then the results can be most damaging.

Responses of the Damaged Self

How does this damaging occur, and what response does the damaged self give to its work? Consider the case of Don. Don's parents wanted him to be a football great. Don's father had played professional football and gave Don a football for his third birthday. Don noticed that there was a single path leading to popularity with his parents and his peers. He decided to give the athletic world all he had. I only came to be his friend in adulthood, yet he confessed to me that all through high school and college he was a dedicated "jock." He sold himself to competition and became reasonably good. Unfortunately, he was never quite good enough to please the two most important people in his cheering squad—his mother and father! Or, at least, as nearly as he could tell, they were never pleased with him. His parents were not strong on affirmation; they were far more likely to remind him he had fumbled the ball in the first quarter than that he had made a touchdown in the fourth quarter.

Don's father actually had a heart attack at one of his high school games and while his father had a history of heart disease, Don couldn't help seeing his own poor game as the cause. After his recovery, the father started attending the games again and would shout near-obscenities at him while he was actually on the playing field. Neither his mother or father approved of anything he did. They did not approve of his poorer athletic showing in college (where the inter-varsity competition was too tough for him). They did not approve of his grades when they dropped below "A+." It was only a matter of time till they did not approve of his fiancée, and so he eloped.

While I was frequent in my affirmation of him, he never seemed to be able to trust that affirmation. His feelings of low self-esteem continue on to the present time just as does his unwillingness to quit competing. He is a highly productive man and yet he sees so little that he does as worthwhile. He is nearly fifty pounds overweight now. He still has an "athlete's blush" at every compliment, which he longs for yet never quite believes. He is an example of all that can happen to self-image when parenthood is crushing and overcorrecting.

As we said in an earlier chapter, parents have almost frightening control over the development of a healthy innate self. Don illustrates that this quantum product was more than adequate to cause his parents to rejoice at all he was accomplishing. Since they never celebrated it, neither did he. Since they viewed him in a limited way, they fashioned his innate self in a limited way.

As a damaged self, Don at least has preserved a willingness to enter into life and participate in it. Bill, another friend of mine, had an equally pressurized childhood. Although he planned to study architecture, he was a talented musician and appeared in many musical events all through school. Other than that, the circumstances were pretty much the same. Since his parents rarely complimented his achievements, but rehearsed his failures regularly, he has grown to manhood with a fear of relationships. He is a talented architect now, yet he seems to have a genuine fear of getting closely involved with anyone around him.

He remains a damaged self in spite of the fact that he produces "great stuff" and all around him affirm the quality of his product. Bill demonstrates one of the observable qualities of damage—he is afraid of relationships. At the beginning of our friendship, he told me how he hoped our friendship would be close because, more than anything else, he wanted and needed a close friend. I was then and am now convinced he really meant what he said. However, my attempts to foster the friendship with dinner invitations, lunches, or other outings were always rejected. His fear of our friendship becoming a judgment or disappointment literally kept our friendship from ever coming to be.

A damaged self often insulates itself from further pain in this way. Such selves are not always as passive as Bill's. Sometimes they take the path of belligerence or arrogance. As we said in a previous chapter, Narcissus is usually inferiority in disguise. Carlton proves the proverb. He often appears haughty. He is as faithful to his church as he could possibly be, but he has never appeared happy there! He seems to be so negative as to have attracted few friends. He appears unloving, but such is not the real case. He does love people, but he feels uncomfortable in expressing his love. He was so injured by his father's indifference to him in early childhood that his own self-perception went begging. But one thing his lifelong experience taught him was that he could keep life at a safe distance by being abrasive at everyone's approach. This has left him a lonely person, but for him loneliness was better than losing.

All such behavior is an evidence that self has been damaged and is coping with its scarred and hurting ego. Low self-esteem, fear of relationships, belligerence, and arrogance are all ways of coping with the great advancing world that is always seeking to move in on us.

Psychological damage can be severe and in many cases it takes years of treatment to straighten out the abused soul to the point where it may take its place in society. If you have experienced some real ego damage, there are some things you can do to help heal yourself. If you have been badly hurt you may need all four of the following steps of healing to get your life working again.

The First Step of Healing: The God-View of Ourselves

First of all, and perhaps foundational to all, is the necessity of getting the God-view of yourself. Who you are is not determined by how you see yourself. You can speak of the more common things that teach you how God sees you; for instance, you are made in His image and likeness. He also gave you this wonderful world to enjoy. He gave you Holy Scripture to teach you of Himself and guide you through the uncharted seas of your future. All these things are beautiful and true, but there is one more lavish proof that you are special to God. The richest meaning of your life is contained in the idea that Christ loved you enough to give His life for you.

In order to capture this view of the loving Christ, you may need to get over your feelings of hostility toward God. At some time in all of our lives we get the feeling that God is against us and that God is unfair to us. Job had these feelings.

I was at ease, but He shattered me,
And He has grasped me by the neck and shaken me to
pieces;
He has also set me up as His target.

His arrows surround me.
Without mercy He splits my kidneys open;
He pours out my gall on the ground.
He breaks through me with breach after breach;
He runs at me like a warrior.
I have sewed sackcloth over my skin,
And thrust my horn in the dust.
My face is flushed from weeping,
And deep darkness is on my eyelids,
Although there is no violence in my hands,
And my prayer is pure.

Job 16:12–17 (NAS)

But until you lay aside such feelings of hostility, you carry on a cynic's rehearsal.

Such a surrender cannot come easily or suddenly. You must rather discipline yourself to communicate with God. If you communicate with God, sooner or later, your conversation will sweeten. Conversation is the key. It is better to be mad at God and tell Him so than not to talk to Him at all.

The God's-eye view of who you are always in time comes back to the idea that you are saved by a living Redeemer. Even Job conceded this when he cried:

I know that my Redeemer lives,
and that in the end he will stand
upon the earth.
And after my skin has been destroyed,
yet in my flesh I will see God.

Job 19:25, 26 (NIV)

In the God's-eye view, Job knew that all his present ugly circumstances were redeemable in time.

Rollo May said that for all of us death is the ultimate pornography. It is mankind's final dirty word. It is the grand, final put-down of self. Yet as God views death, it is not final. It is rather the great transcendence and the whole issue of our worth to God. God thinks so much of us that He made us eternal just as He is. He loves us and wants us forever in His presence.

Of course the whole reason that we can be forever in His presence is that we are the objects of His redeeming love. What a marvelous pier is His cross—a pier strong enough for our salvation and hence our self-worth to rest upon. Stephen Brown calls us to security in who we are: "Your self-esteem is based on the fact that a sovereign God loved you and thought you valuable enough to send His Son to die for you. Once your self-esteem has that basis, almost all other areas are irrelevant."[6]

The basis of sacrifice is love, and His love is a great motivator that should cause you to love yourself. If you live regularly in someone else's high esteem, it is all but impossible for you to live without esteeming yourself.

I often play racquetball with Jim, who is a great athlete. Jim, a young pediatrician, moved to our congregation from the Orient, where his parents once served as Presbyterian missionaries. The first day we played I returned to the locker room soundly defeated. As Jim undressed, I could not help but notice that his torso was crossed by zigzagging scars.

"What happened to you?" I asked.

"I had a kidney transplant," he said rather matter-of-factly.

"Really," I remarked, "Who was the donor?"

"My dad . . . It's funny about my dad," he said wistfully. "We used to quarrel a lot. Then one day I took my last trip on the dialysis machine and Dad and I went into surgery together. You know, after my surgery, I saw all these scars and I thought, 'How ugly.' Then I realized my dad had scars just like mine. Suddenly it seemed to me that these scars were really very beautiful. Does it seem weird to you, pastor?" he asked.

"Not at all . . . go on," I urged.

"Well," he said more slowly, "I never see my dad, even when he's got on a real trim suit, but what I stop and realize that his body bears these same marks. You know what I think now? All those quarrels we had in high school don't mean a thing. He had to love me a lot to carry all these scars. If it wasn't for my dad, I wouldn't be here right now."

The church has traditionally celebrated the stigmata in the hands and feet of Christ. Why have these stigmata been so very important? Because these scars for the church are the primary evidence that we are loved. Cross-love then is the primary basis of our self-esteem.

The Second Step of Healing: Retraining Our Thought Habits

Although you may realize His great love for you from time to time, you still can fall under the burden of stifling low self-esteem. Therefore, you must add to the knowledge that you are special in God's sight, the discipline of retraining your thought habits. Inner self-perceptions are desperately hard to reprogram.

To switch from negative to positive thinking about ourselves is arduous and includes three steps: blockage, substitution, and rehearsal. When Saint Paul encouraged us to "let the peace of Christ rule in your hearts" (Colossians 3:15 NIV), he was saying that the rule of inner peace must have the right to "umpire" all we are (indeed, the meaning of the word *rule* here is "umpire"). An umpire is an official who makes rulings on whether the action of the contest is fair or not.

The inner Christ performs that function and you must hear Him. The peace of God blows the whistle like a game official and says, "That low-esteem thought you have just allowed yourself is simply not fair. It is based, not on any objective truth, but on your negative way of thinking. You should immediately eliminate that thought since it is inconsistent with God's love for you. Further, you should eliminate it on the solid evidence that a score of people who really know you would disagree with it."

This is the inner logic that precedes blockage.

Blockage is the painful process of interrupting your habitual negative thought patterns. This is not easy, because you have trained yourself over years—decades in some cases—to put yourself down. These habit ruts are cut so deep into your psyche that they run without any conscious pilot to direct them. Even when your life is splendid, you can find yourself in the middle of an egoistic self-pity party with no idea how you got there.

Still, blockage can be accomplished if you are willing to garrison your mind and "let the peace of God umpire." Blocking those negative thoughts is the work of constantly patrolling your negativity. You must never cower before this dark and negative, never-ending onslaught of self-recrimination. Emilie Griffin said in another context that we must never run from the dark and menacing circumstances of our lives. She reminds us that darkness comes to strengthen our prayer life and then adds: "Running away from darkness is very human. . . .

"It would be well now to remember, if we can do it without too much spiritual ambition, that the dark way was the way in which the Father led the Son.

"Even in Gethsemane he did not run. He wanted to. He asked for the cup to pass. But he did not run."[7]

Although blockage seems impossible, we must stand against inner negativism. To see ourselves in a new way, we must quit seeing ourselves in the old way.

After blockage comes the second step that I would like to call substitution. Blockage stops the black locomotive; substitution is the switch that puts you on a new track. After laboring under self-recrimination, suddenly you see the real you who has been there all the time. This you is indeed admirable and loved and potentially positive in a wide world of relationships.

In a sense, we all select our own attitudes toward ourselves and our lives. Viktor Frankl reminds us that freedom has a special definition: "Ultimate freedom is man's right to choose his attitude."[8] "Gird up the loins of your mind" (*see* 1 Peter 1:13) and make it serve you—be its master and not its slave. Force it onto the positive track of self-image rather than allowing it to run full throttle on the rails of negativity.

Rehearsal is the last step. Once you have made solid posi-

tive substitutions about the course of your life, then constantly rehearse these new substituted positive images. It is
an oversimplification, but there is much truth in the little tale
called "Bengie Engie." "I think I can" has its best impact in
rehearsal. It is not that everyone who thinks he can, really
can. Some cannot. But the thought itself in every case of
human achievement must precede the deed. Without the rehearsal, nothing comes to be.

A thousand young girls dreamed of Olympic gymnastic
fame. Many thought they could and dreamed of nothing else.
The title could come only to one and Nadia won it. But was
this incessant rehearsal wasted on all the others? Certainly
not. In this "I think I can" way of life, the dream itself became for them the great transcendence. They were so much
more than they ever would have been without that dream.
You can add some reinforcement to your rehearsal of positive
thought patterns. Blockage, substitution, and rehearsal is the
plan for changing negative thinking, but you need a set of
tools for making it all happen. Therefore, let me suggest five
reinforcing disciplines that can be employed to eliminate
negative self-concepts.

1. Prepare spiritually for the day. This can be accomplished by rising early enough to read a devotional passage
and to focus on God. Then in the quiet time that follows, review in writing what you believe to be God's overall plan for
your life, and particularly for this day. Finally, before you
leave the devotional arena, rehearse (commit to memory)
such Bible verses as will help you view the positive qualities
of God's support of your life. There are many fine Scriptures
which emphasize our ability to handle life through God's
power: Philippians 3:14, 4:13, 4:19, 1:6, are such Scriptures.

*2. Never leave your dressing mirror until you are satisfied
that the best criteria for taste and personal neatness have
been achieved.* Your clothes and personal grooming will go a
long way in determining not only how others see you, but
how they relate to you.

3. Force yourself into a positive interchange of some sort with all whom your eyes directly meet. This may be only in the saying of "hello" or "please" and "thank you." It may mean that you need to use some interchange of affirmation or affability as well. But the discipline will need to be thorough if you have established an aloof life-style.

4. *Make all of life a game of names.* Use your name first when meeting someone for the first time, as it is the best encourager for people to respond by sharing their own. As much as possible, use the names of others in all exchanges. Names are the truly magic words. Then keep at the front of your mind the notion that people are nameable, knowable, and special. The remembering of names is a discipline that will win you much admiration.

5. *Practice the art of peripheral praying for those you see but do not have the time or opportunity to talk with.* Peripheral praying draws your world near and closes a circle of manageability around your acquaintances. It makes you a participant in the whole world. Merely seeing others makes you see yourself in a contextual way. This keeps you from insulating yourself and feeling like a social misfit.

Notice that points one and five are "en-static"; that is, these are ways we deal inside ourselves to help heal our damaged feelings. Points two through four are "ek-static." They are points that bring us joy merely because we are making an effort to get outside ourselves and relate. There is no magic in these ideas. Joy ever relates from the "ecstasy" of standing outside ourselves. Thus we escape the littleness of our own world.

The Third Step of Healing: Becoming Productive

The third step in healing your damaged self is the step of becoming productive again. With new product, you take a giant step in the direction of self-esteem. The first and most important part of this is seeing your work in relation to God. If ever you want the best view of what you produce, you must see it this way.

Frank Laubach once saw an enormous dam in which electricity was being generated—or at least the possibility of such generation was there. He asked his host who was showing him the dam, "Here is plenty of water, the turbines are installed, but nothing is being produced—why?" He was told simply, "The valves are closed."

The reason that dam existed was to produce electricity. A similar kind of shutdown can come to your life. Open the valves and let life flow. God will move through your life and there will be product.

Do you remember Snow White's friends going off to the mines each morning? They sang, "Heigh ho, heigh ho, it's off to work we go!" This was the joy of mining. Most miners are not that ecstatic about going off to work. Still, the dwarves were happy. Why? They sang "Heigh ho" for relational reasons. They found joy in their work because their pickaxes dug from the stony mine walls the glittering product of their toil: diamonds.

The song of the dwarves speaks to the wonderful truth penned by Henry van Dyke:

This is the gospel of labor,
ring it, ye bells of the kirk!
The Lord of Love came down from above,
to live with men who work;
This is the rose that He planted,
here in the thorn-curst soil;
Heaven is blest with perfect rest,
but the blessing of Earth is toil.[9]

The Fourth Step of Healing: Identity as Healing

The fourth and final step in the healing of your damaged self has to do with your identity in Christ. This reason passes close to the first step of healing which was the obtaining of God's view of who you are. Still, identity with Christ is more than understanding how God sees you. This step says that at last you have broken free of all concern about yourself. You cannot feel badly about who you are or how good or bad you are. He has become so central in your worldview that you no longer take yourself so seriously. At last you can quit being so self-concerned by wrapping yourself totally in the product that comes from your relationship with Him.

I often marvel at the saints of God. They are usually so Christ-absorbed that they seem to miss the real sense of their own greatness. I think Saint Paul would have been astonished if anyone had told him that his letter to the church at Corinth would one day be a better seller than Aristotle. He lived simply and died simply, thinking mostly of God. "For to me, to live is Christ and to die is gain" (Philippians 1:21 NIV) he stated. Since his identity was his definition, he succeeded without noticing it.

Had he been examined by Abraham Maslow, he would have been pronounced self-actualized. He was not self-absorbed but Christ-absorbed. His cause devoured him. He became unwittingly an all-productive self greater than he would have been, joined to lesser causes. Henri Nouwen said that when you are really bound up in Christ, your successes and failures do indeed lose some of their power over you.

Identity with Christ is the great healer! You will n̄ ̲ong hurt because you are not more celebrated, if your life has an unbroken focus on Him. There is an old hymn that speaks to this wisdom: "Let me lose myself to find it, Lord, in Thee, Let all self be lost—my friends see only Thee!" And, of course, the hymn is based on Jesus' daring challenge, "For whosoever will save his life shall lose it; but whosoever shall lose his life for my sake and the gospel's shall save it" (see Mark 8:35). Neither this song nor Scripture are written to teach us to despise ourselves but to move into a greatness that is free of the bondage of self-concern.

Conclusion

In the face of a thousand popular positivists, each with his own scheme of self-esteem, this is perhaps the final recourse: It is not so important to esteem *our*selves as to love *Him.* When we love Him we shall know that He loved us, even to the giving of His life. We will then be absorbed in such greatness we will not stoop to examine the issue of our own esteem. The healing of damaged selves is bound up in Jesus who attracts the depressed and inferiority-ridden. Those who come to Him, find Him so altogether worthy that they relinquish unnecessary self-concern, lost in the wonder of His greatness.

Afterword

Whatever we do that bends our muscles or taxes our minds—or touches ideas, or lives, or completes the assembly line—all is product. When what we offer our world is appreciated, the world becomes the mirror of our lives.

Perhaps the beginning point is not in the offering of our product, but in the conception of why any particular day has been given to us. The very clock that ticks away the seconds of our lives becomes the altar where we must lay all that we produce from life. In continually producing we make a lot of work for ourselves, but there is no effortless way to real becoming.

My son mowed our lawn from the time he was ten years old till he left home for college. At first he was excited at the response of the pull cord, the whir of the motor, and the geometrics of the new-cut-grass patterns by which he measured his work.

He never complained. He never asked to be excused. It was odd that he even seemed to like doing it. Round and round the yard he pushed the sluggish red machine for the years of green spirals. "Looks nice, huh, Dad?" he would say, finishing the yard. I lived for his boyish smile and the way he surveyed his work and said, "huh, Dad?"

In time his little red shorts—the uniform of his lawn-mowing day—gave way in adolescence to denim cutoffs. His legs lengthened from Fauntleroy to Schwarzenegger. When the green grass had died over a decade of brown autumns, he called me one day to the garage.

"Dad, I have to go away to college now," he advised.

"There are some things you ought to know. This is a lawn mower," he pointed down to the red machine between us. "This is the pull cord. This is the spark plug. You may need this little lever on sluggish mornings . . . it's called a choke."

I looked at him; he was smiling. Could this be the ten-year-old who once said, "Looks nice, huh, Dad?" A moment of guilt passed over me. I had not mowed the lawn in nearly a decade, while he had been busy in the process of his own becoming. His product came week by week as he stacked the bags of clippings at the curb.

Production and becoming always go together. In a decade of making our yard more beautiful, he was making something more important: himself. Now his life yields other kinds of product of a more sophisticated nature. Higher levels of self-esteem demand worthier products. In the product, however, is our becoming. All we shall be, therefore, must remain secret until all we have done has been measured. Then life will be over . . . or will it?

I think not.

Becoming can hardly be the entire subject of our present lives, to be ignored in the next. "Beloved, it doth not yet appear what we shall be" (*see* 1 John 3:2). How true! But let us not waste our days speculating on the issue. The Holy Grail *is* holiest not when we have it but while we pursue it. It is the "getting there" not the "being there" that fills life with meaning; the way not the goal is the glory. Becoming lays its own rails to our future, more finished selves. Becoming is everything.

Source Notes

Chapter One

1. Warren Bennis and Burt Nanus, *Leaders: The Strategies of Taking Charge* (New York: Harper & Row, 1985), p. 89.
2. Walt Disney, cited in Bennis and Nanus, *Leaders*, p. 33.
3. Lao-tzu, cited in Bennis and Nanus, *Leaders*, p. 152.
4. Jacob Bronowski, *The Ascent of Man*, cited in Bennis and Nanus, *Leaders*, p. 187.
5. Ralph W. Neighbour, Jr., "The Urbanization of the Earth," *Future Church*, Ralph W. Neighbour, Jr., comp. (Nashville: Broadman, 1980), p. 9.
6. Edward Hays, "The Stranger's Bargain," *Twelve and One-Half Keys* (Easton, Kansas: Forest Peace, 1983), pp. 51–60.
7. Harry Emerson Fosdick, *The Meaning of Prayer* (Nashville: Abingdon, 1982), p. 49.
8. George Eliot, cited in Fosdick, *The Meaning of Prayer*, p. 61.

Chapter Two

1. Alexis de Tocqueville, *Democracy in America*, Vol. 1 (New York: Vintage Books, 1945), pp. 27–28, cited in James MacGregor Burns, *Leadership* (New York: Harper & Row, 1979), p. 81.

2. George Washington Plunkitt, cited in W. L. Riordan, *Plunkitt of Tammany Hall* (New York: McClure, Phillips, 1905), pp. 33–34, cited in Burns, *Leadership*, pp. 311–312.
3. Cited in Burns, *Leadership*, p. 251.
4. Bernard M. Bass, *Leadership, Psychology and Organizational Behavior* (New York: Harper & Brothers, 1960), p. 299, cited in Burns, *Leadership*, p. 100.

Chapter Three

1. Lincoln Kirstein, cited in Warren Bennis and Burt Nanus, *Leaders: The Strategies of Taking Charge* (New York: Harper & Row, 1985), p. 31.
2. Henry Ford, cited in Theodore Levitt, *The Marketing Imagination* (New York: Free Press, Macmillan, 1983), p. 142.
3. Robert Frost, cited in Paul W. Powell, *The Complete Disciple* (Wheaton, Ill.: Victor Books, 1984), p. 50.
4. Calvin Miller, "I-Ness," *When the Aardvark Parked on the Ark* (San Francisco: Harper & Row, 1984), p. 150.
5. Robert Ardrey, *The Territorial Imperative*, cited in Robert H. Schuller, *Self-Love* (Old Tappan, N.J.: Revell, 1969), p. 15.

Chapter Four

1. Saul Bellow, *Humboldt's Gift*, cited in Paul W. Powell, *The Complete Disciple* (Wheaton, Ill.: Victor Books, 1984), p. 47.
2. Andy Warhol, cited in Powell, *The Complete Disciple*, p. 48.
3. James MacGregor Burns, *Leadership* (New York: Harper & Row, 1979), p. 1.
4. Lee Iacocca, *Iacocca: An Autobiography*, with William Novak (New York: Bantam, 1984), p. 47.

5. Richard J. Foster, *Freedom of Simplicity* (New York: Harper & Row, 1981), p. 91.
6. Dr. James Dobson, *Hide or Seek* (Old Tappan, N.J.: Revell, 1974), p. 150.
7. Calvin Miller, *Transcendental Hesitation*, p. 126.
8. Dobson, *Hide or Seek*, p. 28.
9. Lee Bickmore, cited in Powell, *The Complete Disciple*, pp. 61–62.
10. John White, *The Race* (Downers Grove, Ill.: Inter-Varsity, 1984), p. 176.
11. Cited in Lewis Smedes, *How Can It Be All Right When Everything Is All Wrong?* (San Francisco: Harper & Row, 1982), p. 20.
12. Rollo May, *The Courage to Create* (New York: Bantam, 1980), p. 27.

Chapter Five

1. Cited in Rollo May, *The Courage to Create* (New York: Bantam, 1980) p. 72.
2. John Osborne, *Luther* (New York: New American Library, 1963).
3. Henri J.M. Nouwen, *Out of Solitude* (Notre Dame, Indiana: Ave Maria, 1981), p. 23.
4. M. Scott Peck, *People of the Lie* (New York: Simon and Schuster, 1983), pp. 47–59.
5. Alan Loy McGinnis, *Bringing Out the Best in People* (Minneapolis: Augsburg, 1985), p. 163.
6. Harrison Salisbury, *Success Magazine*, February 1986, p. 75.
7. Nathaniel Branden, *The Psychology of Romantic Love* (Los Angeles: J.P. Tarcher, 1980), p. 61, cited in McGinnis, *Bringing Out the Best in People*, p. 162.

Chapter Six

1. Samuel Beckett, *Waiting for Godot* (New York: Grove, 1954).
2. Rene Dubos, *Celebrations of Life* (New York: McGraw-Hill, 1981), pp. 100–101.
3. Nikolai Lenin, cited in Klaus Bockmuehl, *The Challenge of Marxism* (Downers Grove, Ill.: Inter-Varsity, 1980), p. 35.
4. Judith Deem Dupree, "Chiseler," *Going Home* (Palm Springs, Calif.: Ronald N. Haynes Publishers, 1984), p. 17.
5. Booker T. Washington, *Up From Slavery.*
6. Don Marquis, "The Lesson of the Moth," cited in Warren Bennis and Burt Nanus, *Leaders: The Strategies for Taking Charge* (New York: Harper & Row, 1985), pp. 53–54.
7. James Kavanaugh, "I'm Gonna Sit Here," *Laughing Down Lonely Canyons* (San Francisco: Harper & Row, 1984), p. 31.
8. Nevil Shute, *On The Beach* (New York: William Morrow, 1957).
9. Paul Tournier, cited by Robert Banks, *The Tyranny of Time* (Downers Grove, Ill.: Inter-Varsity, 1983), p. 210.
10. Ronald Dunn, *The Faith Crisis* (Wheaton, Ill.: Tyndale, 1984), p. 14.
11. C.S. Lewis, *A Grief Observed* (New York: Bantam, 1980), p. 43.
12. Flannery O'Connor, *The Violent Bear It Away* (New York: Farrar, Straus & Giroux, 1955), p. 8.
13. Paul E. Billheimer, *Don't Waste Your Sorrows* (Fort Washington, Pa.: Christian Literature Crusade, 1977), p. 43.

Chapter Seven

1. Richard E. Ecker, *The Stress Myth* (Downers Grove, Ill.: Inter-Varsity, 1985), pp. 9–10.

2. L. Mumford, *Technics and Civilization*, cited in Robert Banks, *The Tyranny of Time* (Downers Grove, Ill.: Inter-Varsity, 1983), p. 97.
3. G.A. Woodcock, "The Tyranny of the Clock," *An Introduction to Social Science*, cited in Banks, *The Tyranny of Time*, p. 39.
4. Eugene H. Peterson, *Earth & Altar* (Downers Grove, Ill.: Inter-Varsity, 1985), p. 13.
5. Cited in Warren Bennis and Burt Nanus, *Leaders: The Strategies of Taking Charge* (New York: Harper & Row, 1985), p. 56.
6. Earl D. Wilson, *The Discovered Self* (Downers Grove, Ill.: Inter-Varsity, 1985), p. 17.
7. Oscar Hammerstein II, "The Farmer and the Cowman Should Be Friends," *Oklahoma* (New York: Chappell and Co.).
8. Thomas A. Harris, M.D., *I'm OK, You're OK* (New York: Avon, 1982).
9. Peter Shaffer, *Amadeus* (New York: Harper & Row, 1981).
10. Lee Iacocca, *Iacocca: An Autobiography*, with William Novak (New York: Bantam, 1984), p. 38.
11. Ibid.
12. Theodore Roosevelt, quoted by Ted W. Engstrom with Robert C. Larson, *Motivation to Last a Lifetime* (Grand Rapids, Mich.: Zondervan, 1984), pp. 75–76.
13. Frances Hodgson Burnett, *Little Lord Fauntleroy* (Harmondsworth, Middlesex, England: Puffin Books, 1981), p. 115.

Chapter Eight

1. Hamlet, act 1, sc. 3, lines 82–84.
2. James MacGregor Burns, *Leadership* (New York: Harper & Row, 1979), pp. 56–68.
3. Ibid., p. 105.
4. Ibid., pp. 102–105.
5. Tennessee Williams, *The Glass Menagerie*.

Chapter Nine

1. Warren Bennis and Burt Nanus, *Leaders: The Strategies of Taking Charge* (New York: Harper & Row, 1985), pp. 70, 71.
2. Ernest Hemingway, "Today is Friday."
3. Franky Schaeffer, *The Wittenburg Door.*
4. Earl D. Wilson, *The Discovered Self* (Downers Grove, Ill.: Inter-Varsity, 1985), p. 26.
5. Bernard Bangley, *Growing in His Image* (Wheaton, Ill.: Shaw Pub., 1983), p. 34.
6. Emilie Griffin, *Clinging* (San Francisco: Harper & Row, 1984), p. 23.
7. Wilson, *The Discovered Self,* p. 7.
8. Bennis and Nanus, *Leaders,* p. 76.

Chapter Ten

1. Fyodor Dostoyevsky, *Notes from Underground,* trans. with an introduction by Jessie Coulson (Middlesex, England: Penguin Books, Ltd., 1982), p. 25.
2. Studs Terkel, *Talking to Myself* (New York: Pantheon, 1984), pp. 23–24.
3. Judith Deem Dupree, "Tangent," *Going Home* (Palm Springs, Calif.: Ronald N. Haynes Publishers, 1984), p. 21.
4. Victor Hugo, *The Hunchback of Notre Dame.*
5. Buckminster Fuller, *Saturday Review/World.*
6. Stephen Brown, *If God Is in Charge* (Nashville: Nelson, 1983), p. 116.
7. Emilie Griffin, *Clinging* (San Francisco: Harper & Row, 1984), pp. 24–25.
8. Viktor Frankl, cited in Fred Smith, *You and Your Network* (Waco, Texas: Word Books, 1984), p. 20.
9. Henry van Dyke, cited in Edward Hays, *Secular Sanctity* (Easton, Kansas: Forest Peace, 1984), p. 35.